Charts

OF

Ancient and Medieval Church History

Books in the Zondervan*Charts* Series

Charts

OF

Ancient and Medieval Church History

John D. Hannah

ZONDERVAN™

GRAND RAPIDS, MICHIGAN 49530

ZONDERVAN™

Charts of Ancient and Medieval Church History
Copyright © 2001 by John David Hannah

Requests for information should be addressed to:

Zondervan, *Grand Rapids, Michigan 49530*

Library of Congress Cataloging-in-Publication Data

Hannah, John D.
    Charts of ancient and medieval church history / John D. Hannah.
        p. cm.
        ISBN 0-310-23316-X (softcover)
        1. Church history—Chronology—Charts, diagrams, etc. I. Title.
BR149 .H33 2001
270'.02'02—dc21   2001026576

Interior design by Todd Sprague

Printed in the United States of America

01 02 03 04 05 06 /❖ VG/ 10 9 8 7 6 5 4 3 2 1

To my daughters, Rebecca Ruth Hasselbach and Nancy Leigh Jones,
this work is affectionately dedicated. For years of traveling in summer
ministries, they sacrificed space for things so Dad could take boxes
of charts for his students. They called them his "other children."
My daughters are everything and more than any parent can imagine.
They have been kind and caring. They saw beyond a busy man
who often forgot the duty of understanding to see
one who deeply loved (and loves) them.

101817

Acknowledgments

Many debts are incurred in the writing of materials of every kind. For a patient wife, who was always kind and sympathetic, words are not sufficient to express my gratitude. To the institution that I have served for many years, Dallas Theological Seminary, I recognize that this project would not have been possible without its generous support and encouragement. The audio-visual department has worked with me for nearly three decades, creating materials for my classroom presentations. Many of those tools appear in this volume. The staff people of Mosher and Turpin libraries were always kind and resourceful. The students at the seminary were helpful in the development of each chart as they provided valuable feedback in the context of the classroom. Special thanks goes to one student in particular, Brian Matz, my teaching assistant. His interest and efforts from a technical viewpoint made this volume possible. Lastly, the editors at Zondervan who conceived the project and provided a professionalism beyond my abilities are owed a significant thank-you as well.

Contents

Charts of Ancient and Medieval Church History

The value of history has fallen on tough times in contemporary culture. Postmoderns have demonstrated a tendency to disregard the past as a useless and even debilitating relic, something akin to unwanted dreams and painful experiences. Learning from the collective wisdom of the ages seems of little value in an era where technology and the sciences receive the most support from government; consequently, the arts and humanities are marginalized. We seem determined to improve our outward circumstances while allowing the inner life to decay. Great literature is not read and cherished, cultural values are nullified through the ever-changing excitement of the merely transitory, and life is tyrannized by captivating trivia. A society without a knowledge of its past is one without hope, cursed with the perception that an endless array of passing fads is meaningful. What we seem to prize most is the stuff of future garage sales, the emptiness of preoccupation with athleticism, the spiral of increased debt, and the phantom of deep relationships shattered by broken promises.

At least in part, the contemporary church seems to have imbibed the culture more than resisted its largely unbiblical values. This can be seen in the lack of awareness the Christian has of his or her heritage. The average Christian is, by and large, historically illiterate. With some sense of discomfort they may be enticed to articulate a vague awareness of Martin Luther or John Calvin, yet there seems to be little, if any, understanding that the Christian faith draws on a rich heritage that is centuries in its development. Part of the problem, if truth be told, is that in many of our educational institutions and churches Christians are not being grounded in their heritage.

This brings me to the purpose of preparing this volume, and two subsequent ones, on the history of the Christian church. Before one bemoans the situation too loudly, or at least too incessantly, he ought to endeavor to do something about it. What I have provided are tools for the teaching of our heritage: various charts, diagrams, and maps, together with explanatory captions, unfolding the history of the church. Included with the book is a CD-ROM Powerpoint presentation, which enhances the use of each teaching tool.

Introduction
Church History in a Nutshell

A Panoramic View of Christian History

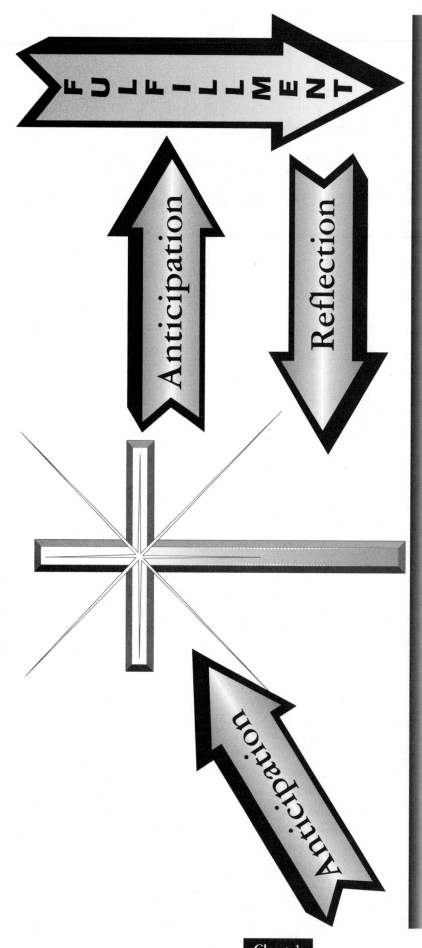

FULFILLMENT

Anticipation

Reflection

Anticipation

The Cross

Creation → → Re-Creation

Chart 1

For the Christian, Jesus Christ is the center of all history. History contains two grand events from a divine perspective: (1) the coming of Christ to redeem his people and (2) the return of Christ to claim his people, judge the world, and reign as King in a new heaven and new earth forever. The time before the first coming of Christ, the Old Testament era, was an age of shadows because it anticipated Christ through promises and ceremonies; the time after Christ until his return is an age of reflection and anticipation. When Christ returns, all of God's promises for humankind and the earth will be fulfilled.

The Meaning of Universal History:
God's Glory Revealed, Redemption Accomplished

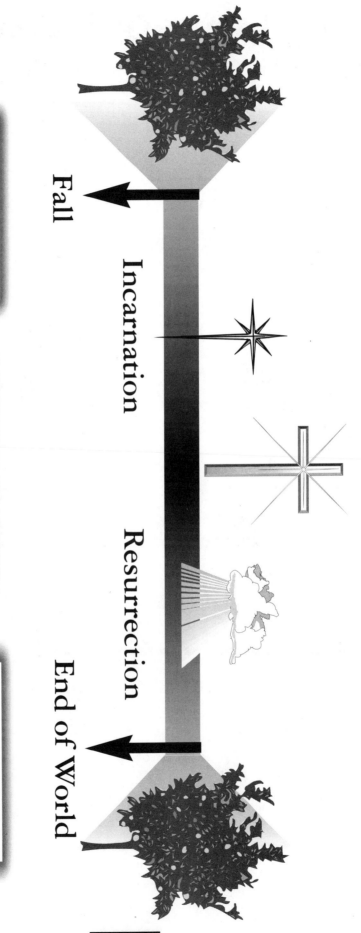

Fall

Incarnation

Resurrection

End of World

Preparation for Redemption

Purchase of Redemption

Accomplishment of Redemption

The story line of history is redemption: revealed, accomplished, and applied. The world began in a garden paradise and will end in one, though it has been temporarily disfigured by a terrible fall through Adam. The restoration of the creation was predicted in the Old Testament, accomplished in the work of Jesus Christ, and will be applied finally and ultimately in the creation of a new garden.

Chart 2

A Summary of Church History

Theme: The Growth of the Kingdom of God in the Kingdom of Man

Emergence of the
Apostles' Doctrine

Restoration of the
Apostles' Doctrine

Semi-Augustinianism,
Semi-Pelagianism, and
Sacramentalism

Enlightenment of
Modern Religious
Thought

A.D. 33

Genesis 3

First Century

Sixteenth Century

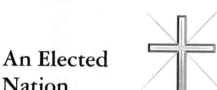

An Elected
Nation

A Gathered
Church

Period of
Anticipation

Period of Reflection
and Anticipation

Fulfillment

The centuries between the comings of Christ comprise the history of the church, promised in shadowed form to Abraham, the father of the faithful of all ages. Our understanding of history has been shaped by Augustine's insight that God is gathering out of the kingdom of man a kingdom purchased by God's Son. The epoch between the two advents has witnessed two periods in which the kingdom of God has made marked progress and two eras in which the kingdom of man has seemingly overshadowed it. The initial several centuries witnessed the expansion and triumph of the church, only to be blighted in the late medieval period by theological confusion and error. The Reformation was an outstanding era of the renewal of the church; recent centuries give evidence of the ebbing of that influence.

Chart 3

The Divisions of History

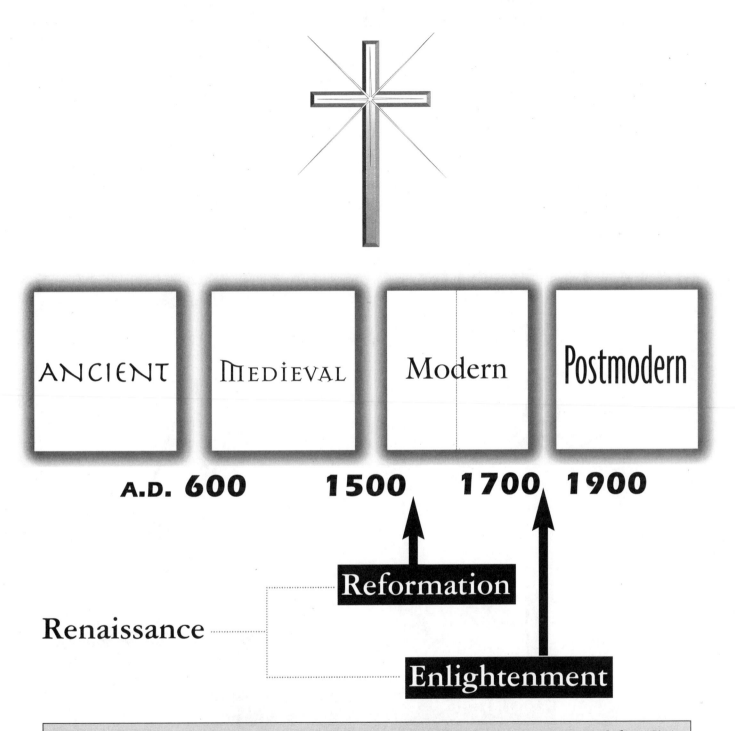

ANCIENT   MEDIEVAL   Modern   Postmodern

A.D. **600**   **1500**   **1700** **1900**

Reformation

Renaissance

Enlightenment

The history of the church through the centuries can be divided into four parts: the ancient period (from Christ to the decline of the Roman Empire), the medieval period (from the Merovingian kings in the West and Justinian in the East to the rise of the Renaissance), the modern period (from the Renaissance to the demise of the Enlightenment (subdivided into two parts—the early modern period, dominated by the religious conservatism of the Reformation, and the late modern period, dominated by the intellectual optimism of the Enlightenment), and the postmodern period, which began about 1900 in Europe and post-World War II in America and continues to the present day.

Chart 4

A Protestant View of Church History

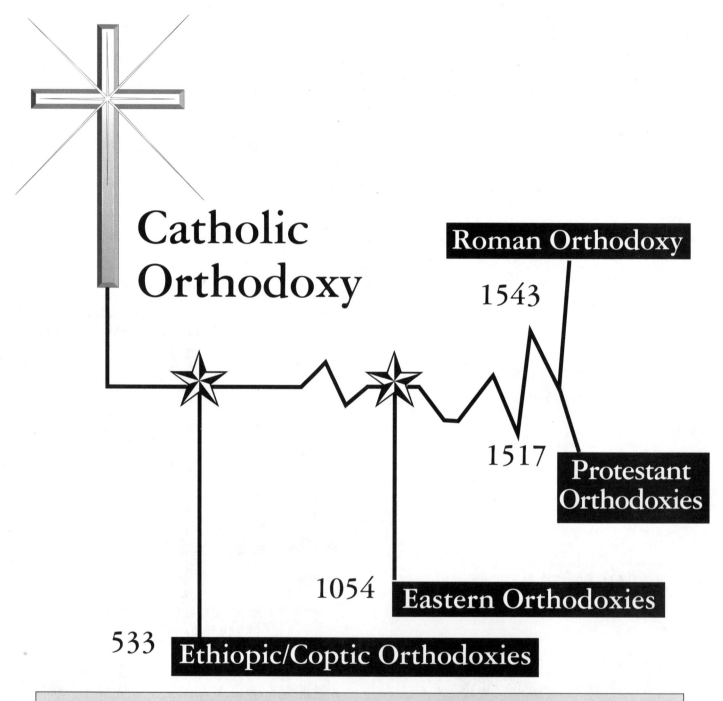

Catholic Orthodoxy

Roman Orthodoxy

1543

1517

Protestant Orthodoxies

1054 Eastern Orthodoxies

533 Ethiopic/Coptic Orthodoxies

Though various religious traditions would diagram the history of the past twenty centuries differently, my approach is that of historic conservative Protestantism. In my view, the church remained essentially orthodox for thirteen or more centuries. Then in the centuries immediately prior to the Reformation the church began to decay, and the need for renewal became painfully evident. While the need for change was generally recognized, the nature of the change brought division in the church. Both Protestantism and Roman Catholicism emerged in the sixteenth century as renewal movements (along with several others).

Chart 5

The Ancient Period
of Church History
(from Christ to 600)

The History of the Church:
The Ancient Period

Age of the Apostles	Age of the Earliest Church Fathers	Age of the Apologists	Age of the Theologians

A.D. **100**   **150**   **300**   **600**

The ancient period divides into four parts: the age of the apostles (from Christ to the end of the first century), the age of the earliest church fathers (writers from the first decades of the second century whose literary tone was pastoral rather than polemical), the age of the apologists (polemical writers who in the face of significant persecution defended the church against a variety of opponents), and the age of the theologians (from the triumph of Christianity to the demise of the Roman Empire in the West).

Chart 6

Prominent Cities in the Eastern Mediterranean

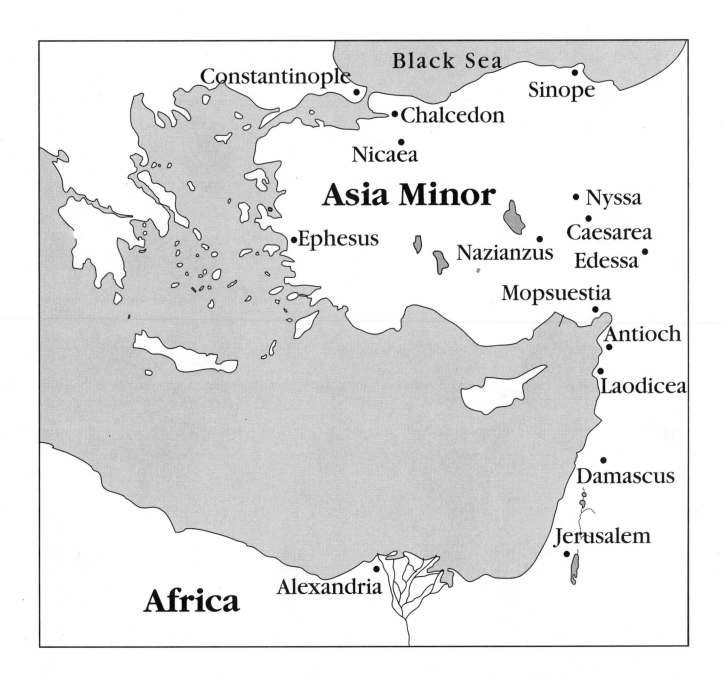

Christianity began in Palestine and spread rapidly throughout the Near East and the Eastern Mediterranean.

Chart 7

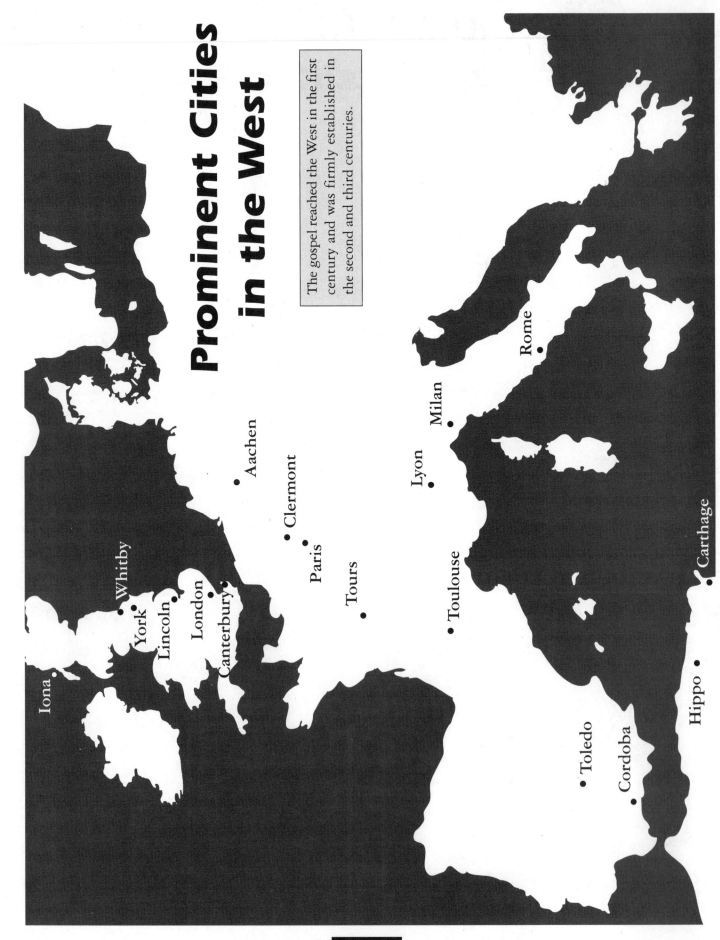

Prominent Cities in the West

The gospel reached the West in the first century and was firmly established in the second and third centuries.

Iona

Whitby

York

Lincoln

London

Canterbury

Aachen

Clermont

Paris

Tours

Lyon

Milan

Rome

Toulouse

Carthage

Toledo

Cordoba

Hippo

Chart 8

The Age of the Apostles
(from Christ to 100)

The Setting of the Church

GALATIANS 4:4

When the time had fully come,
God sent his Son...

THE INFLUENCE OF ROME
POLITICAL

THE INFLUENCE OF GREECE
INTELLECTUAL

THE INFLUENCE OF THE JEWS
RELIGIOUS

The world to which Jesus Christ came and in which the church was born was one that God had uniquely prepared. We can view this through three lenses: (1) the Romans dominated the world, bringing an era of peace, (2) the Greeks gave the world a common language, and (3) the Jews expected the coming of the Anointed One, though they viewed the Messiah as a political figure rather than a spiritual redeemer.

Chart 9

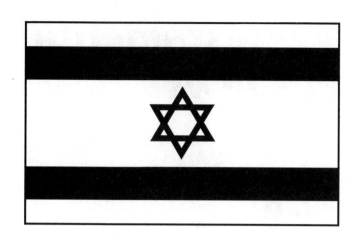

The History of Israel:
The Intertestamental Era

The Old Testament Era

—— 435/432 B.C. —————— MALACHI

The "Silent Years"

JOHN THE BAPTIST ———— 5/4 B.C. ——

The New Testament Era

The period between the end of the Old Testament era and the beginning of the New Testament era (the intertestamental era) is sometimes called the "silent years"—not because so little transpired but because God sent no writing prophets after Malachi until the writers of the Gospels. The revelation of the angel to the parents of John the Baptist, the forerunner of Christ, marks out the renewal of God's revelation to his people, as well as its culmination in Christ.

Chart 10

History of the Intertestamental Era and the Jews

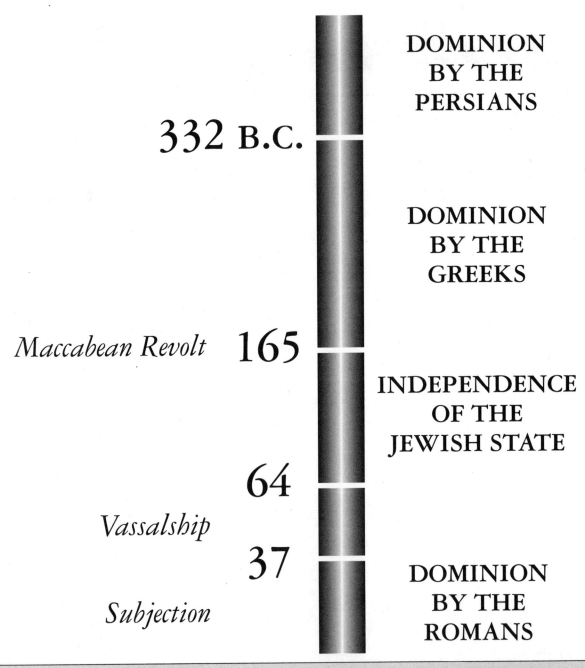

DOMINION BY THE PERSIANS

332 B.C.

DOMINION BY THE GREEKS

Maccabean Revolt 165

INDEPENDENCE OF THE JEWISH STATE

64

Vassalship

37

Subjection

DOMINION BY THE ROMANS

The Jews longed for the Messiah, but expected him to be a military figure who would bring a political deliverance to the nation. God's threatened judgments for disobedience had found fulfillment in the Babylonian destruction of Judah in 586 B.C. A remnant returned under later Persian kings, but only as a subjected people. The Greeks, beginning with Alexander the Great, dominated Palestine and imposed a Hellenistic culture, which precipitated the Maccabean revolt and the reestablishment of the nation. With the coming of the Romans, the hand of oppression settled on the Jews once again. In the days prior to Christ's birth, the Jews longed for a new redemption from their oppression, now not from the Greeks but from the Romans.

Chart 11

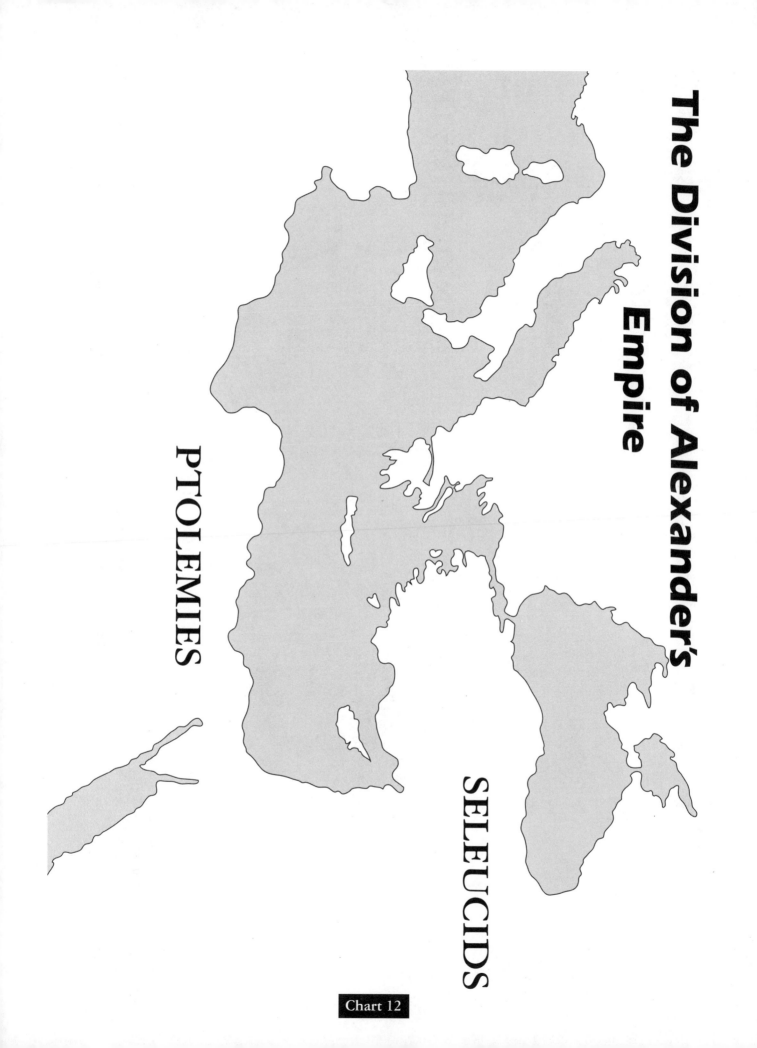

The Division of Alexander's Empire

PTOLEMIES

SELEUCIDS

Chart 12

The Maccabean Revolt

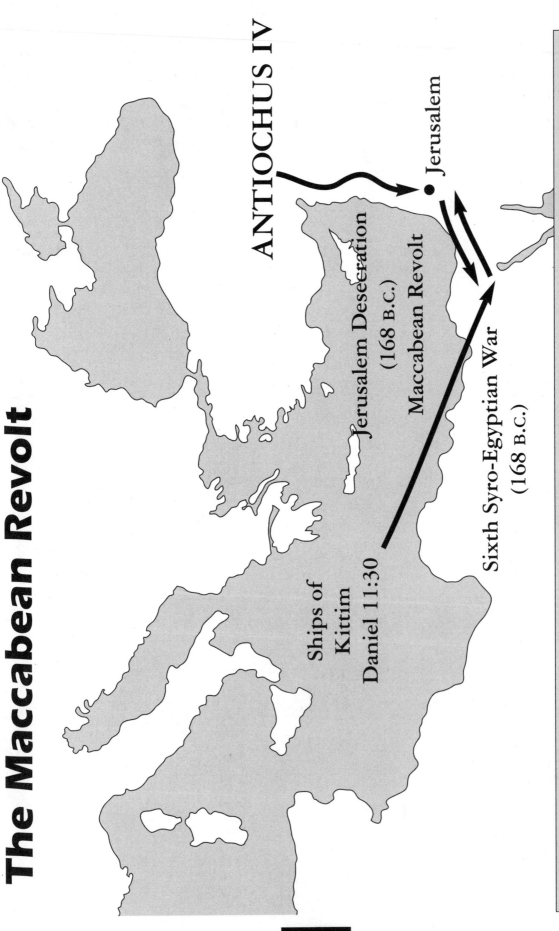

ANTIOCHUS IV

Jerusalem

Jerusalem Desecration
(168 B.C.)
Maccabean Revolt

Ships of
Kittim
Daniel 11:30

Sixth Syro-Egyptian War
(168 B.C.)

Realizing that his kingdom was threatened, Seleucid ruler Antiochus IV Epiphanes retreated from Egypt when the Ptolemies formed military alliances with Rome. Therefore, Antiochus determined to build a buffer state between him and the Egyptians. He ruthlessly imposed Hellenistic culture on the Jewish population, which led to the Maccabean revolt. The Jews established a sovereign state, but increasingly felt the encroachment of the Roman Empire in the East.

Chart 13

THE
LIFE
OF
JESUS
CHRIST

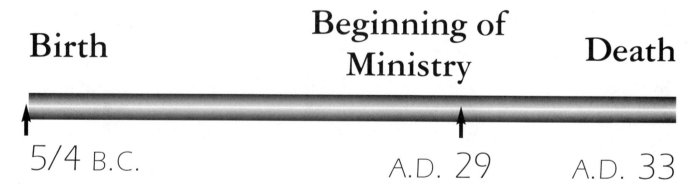

Birth	Beginning of Ministry	Death
5/4 B.C.	A.D. 29	A.D. 33

Jesus Christ came into this world prior to the death of Herod the Great in 4 B.C. If scholars are correct that Christ was crucified in A.D. 33, then he began his ministry about A.D. 29. Luke tells us that Christ began his public ministry at about the age of thirty (3:23).

Chart 14

Palestine in Christ's Day

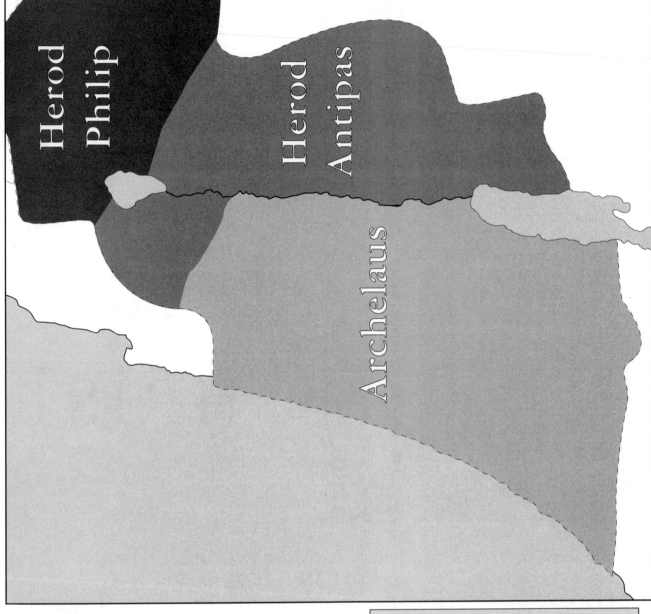

Herod Philip

Herod Antipas

Archelaus

The Territory of Herod the Great

The Territorial Allotment to Herod's Sons

In Christ's day Palestine was ruled by three sons of Herod the Great. Archelaus ruled over Judea and Samaria; Herod Antipas ruled over Galilee and Perea (east of the Jordan); Herod Philip II ruled the areas north and northeast of the Sea of Galilee. After Archelaus was deposed, Rome appointed governors to rule—Pilate being among them. Herod Antipas, called "that fox" by Jesus, divorced his wife to marry his brother's wife, Herodias. Herod Philip built a city (Caesarea Philippi) at the foot of Mount Hermon, naming it after the emperor and himself. There, in a center of pagan worship, Jesus asked his disciples, "Who do you say I am?"

Chart 15

Politics of Palestine in Christ's Day

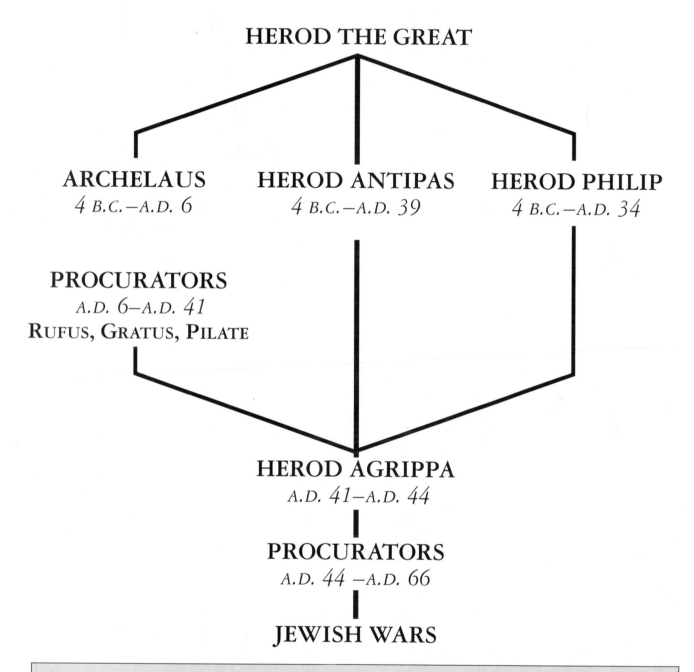

HEROD THE GREAT

ARCHELAUS
4 B.C.–A.D. 6

HEROD ANTIPAS
4 B.C.–A.D. 39

HEROD PHILIP
4 B.C.–A.D. 34

PROCURATORS
A.D. 6–A.D. 41
RUFUS, GRATUS, PILATE

HEROD AGRIPPA
A.D. 41–A.D. 44

PROCURATORS
A.D. 44 –A.D. 66

JEWISH WARS

Christ was born during the reign of a Roman-appointed king, the Jews having lost their sovereignty in 68 B.C. In 37 B.C. matters grew worse when Herod the Great, an Idumean, became king. Though he left a legacy of magnificent buildings, including the renovation of the temple, he was a cruel, demented monarch. His realm was divided among three sons who played a key role in the early story of Christ and the church. Archelaus was cruel, even by Roman standards, and was replaced by a series of governors appointed from Rome. Herod Antipas governed Galilee and the area east of the Jordan. Herod Philip II ruled the region north and northeast of the Sea of Galilee. After their deaths, Herod Agrippa I ruled the consolidated areas.

Chart 16

The Beginning of the Church

April 3rd April 5th May 24th → A.D. 33	Death of Christ Resurrection of Christ Day of Pentecost
A.D. 46–48	First Missionary Journey
A.D. 49–52	Second Missionary Journey
A.D. 53–57	Third Missionary Journey
A.D. 60–62	First Roman Imprisonment
A.D. 67–68	Second Roman Imprisonment
A.D. 70	Destruction of Jerusalem

Details about the beginning and expansion of the church in the first century are largely available through the writings of Luke. Though debated among scholars, it is believed that Christ was crucified on Passover in the year A.D. 33. Fifty days from that day is the Feast of Pentecost. A new era began with the coming of the Spirit in Acts 2, and the "age of shadows" ended. The missionary journeys of Paul span from the late 40s to the late 50s.

Chart 17

Paul's First Missionary Journey

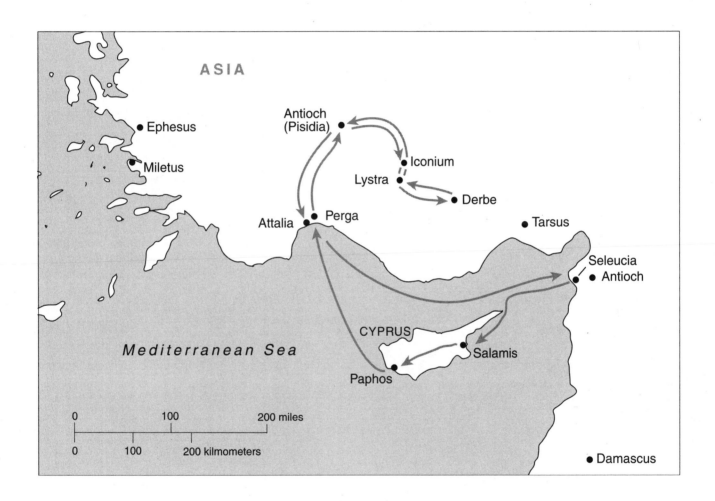

ASIA

Ephesus

Miletus

Antioch (Pisidia)

Iconium

Lystra

Derbe

Attalia • Perga

Tarsus

Seleucia
• Antioch

CYPRUS

Mediterranean Sea

Salamis

Paphos

0   100   200 miles

0   100   200 kilmometers

• Damascus

The book of Acts relates the story of the spread of the church from Jerusalem to the center of the Roman Empire, triumphing over various forms of opposition. The book covers the initial thirty years of the church's history. The focus is on the apostle Paul, the Apostle to the Gentiles. The first missionary journey, across Cyprus and into Asia Minor, was as fruitful as it was difficult. The missionary teams revisited the newly established churches before returning to Antioch in Syria.

Chart 18

Paul's Second Missionary Journey

The second missionary journey took Paul and his companions across Asia Minor to Troas, where the Macedonian vision called them into eastern Europe. They were successful in establishing several churches, some to whom Paul subsequently wrote letters, then crossed the Aegean Sea to Ephesus before embarking for Caesarea in Palestine.

Chart 19

Paul's Third Missionary Journey

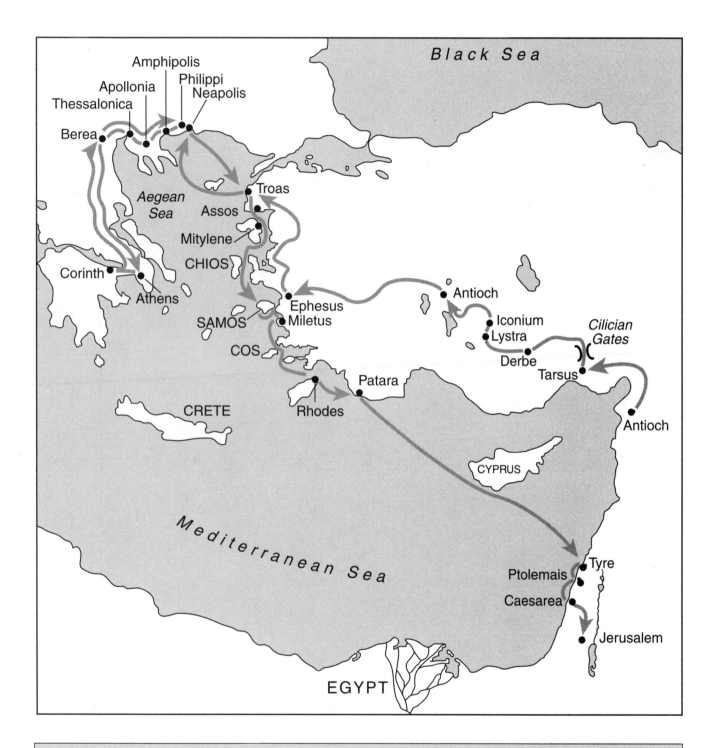

The third journey took Paul along much the same route as the previous missionary endeavor, revisiting the churches and undertaking lengthy periods of ministry in Corinth and Ephesus. He returned to Palestine, where he was arrested in Jerusalem and imprisoned in Caesarea for two years.

Chart 20

Paul's Journey to Rome

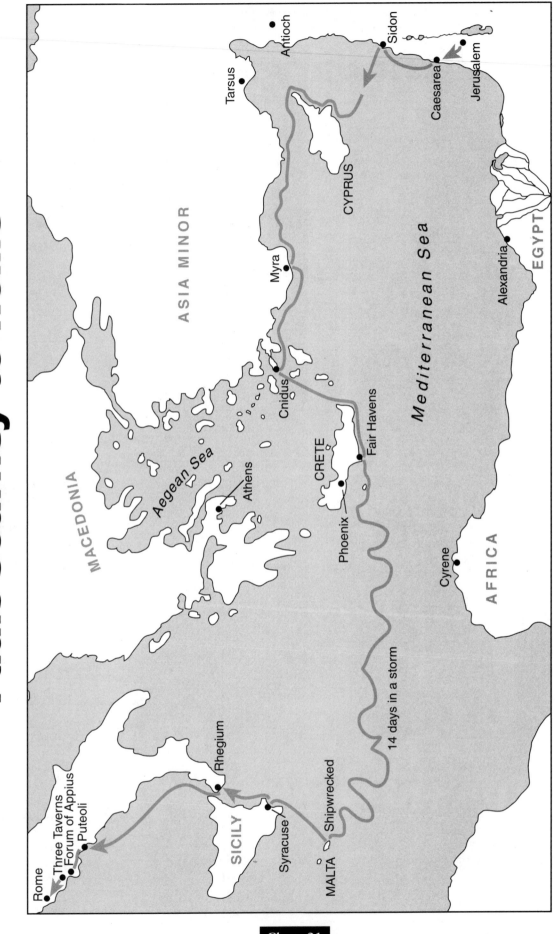

The latter chapters of Acts record Paul's journey to Rome, where he was placed under house arrest and awaited trial.

Chart 21

Paul's Release Journeys

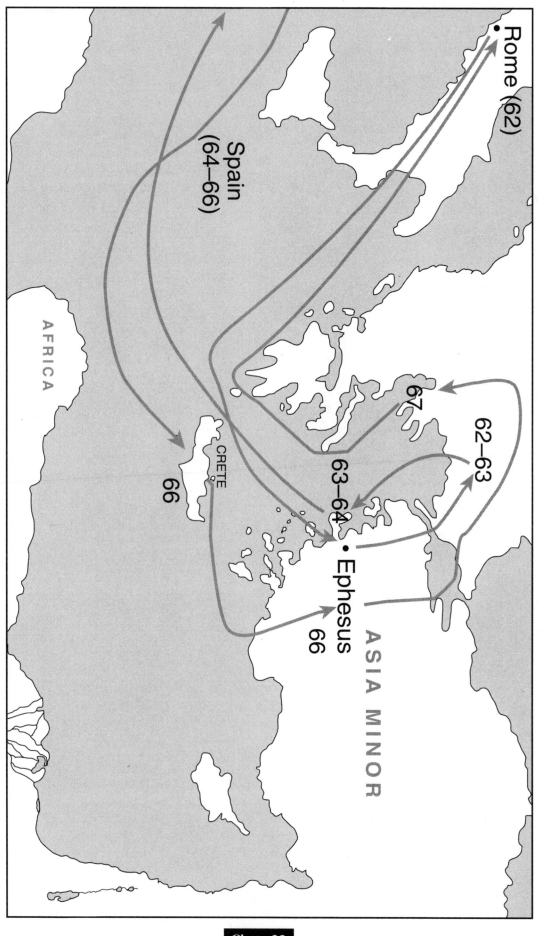

Rome (62)

Spain
(64–66)

AFRICA

CRETE
66

67

62–63

63–64

• Ephesus
66

ASIA MINOR

It is believed that Paul was released from his initial Roman imprisonment, perhaps when his Jewish accusers failed to press charges. He is thought to have traveled to the end of the world of that day. On his return he evangelized the island of Crete, leaving Titus there to organize the churches, and was later arrested in Macedonia. From there he was taken to Rome, where he was martyred.

Chart 22

The Diaspora and the Churches of the First Century

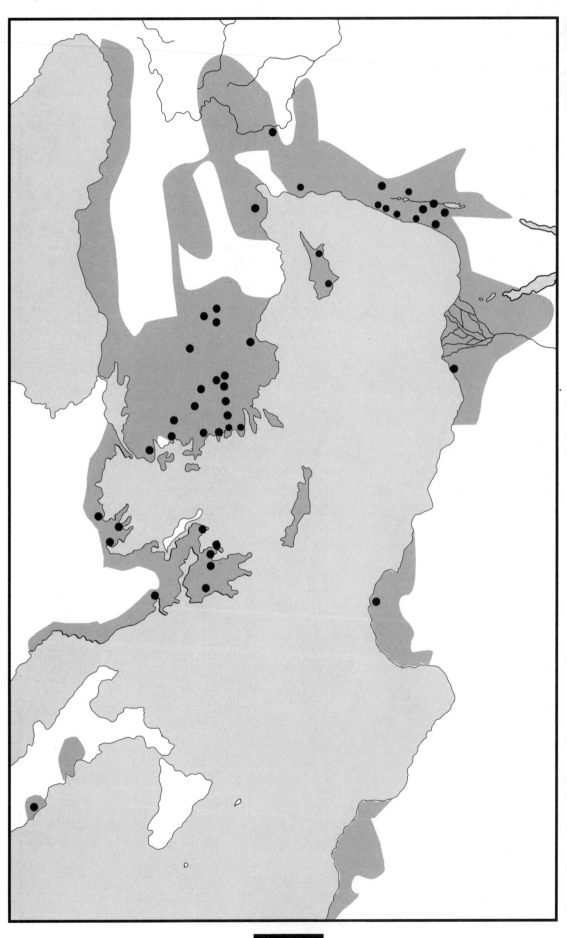

The New Testament indicates that Paul went first to the synagogues to herald the gospel and then turned to the Gentiles when faced with hostility. The earliest churches developed in this manner in places such as Ephesus and Corinth. Paul also took advantage of the network of excellent Roman roads that interconnected the major cities as he and others spread the message of Christ.

Chart 23

The Age of the
Earliest Church Fathers
(from 100 to 150)

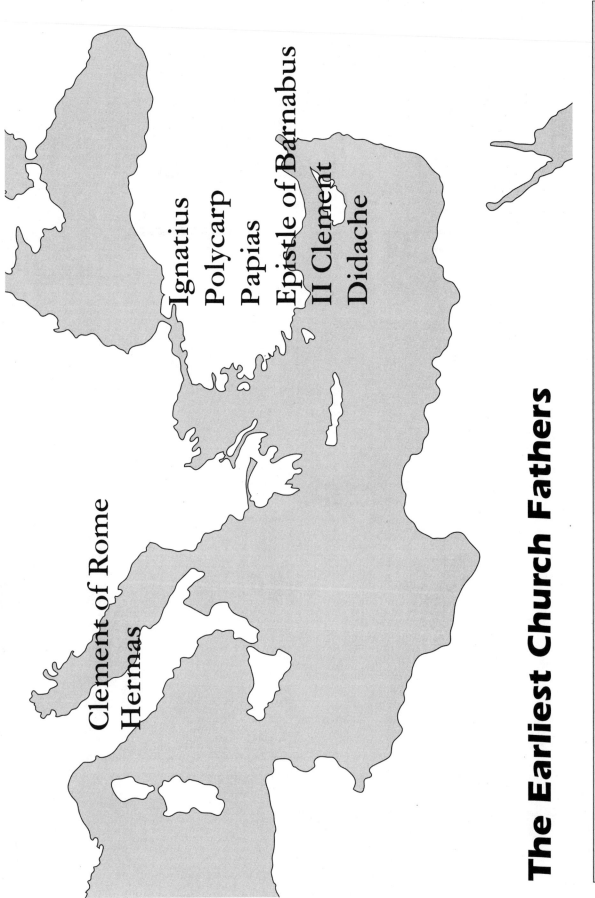

Ignatius
Polycarp
Papias
Epistle of Barnabus
II Clement
Didache

Clement of Rome
Hermas

The Earliest Church Fathers

The writers immediately after (or perhaps overlapping) the apostles produced a body of literature that singles them out as unique. Most of these writers and writings were from the eastern Mediterranean area. They employed the Greek language, the universal language of their day. Their writings were not as strident or polemical in tone as subsequent authors.

Chart 24

The History of the Rise of the Episcopacy

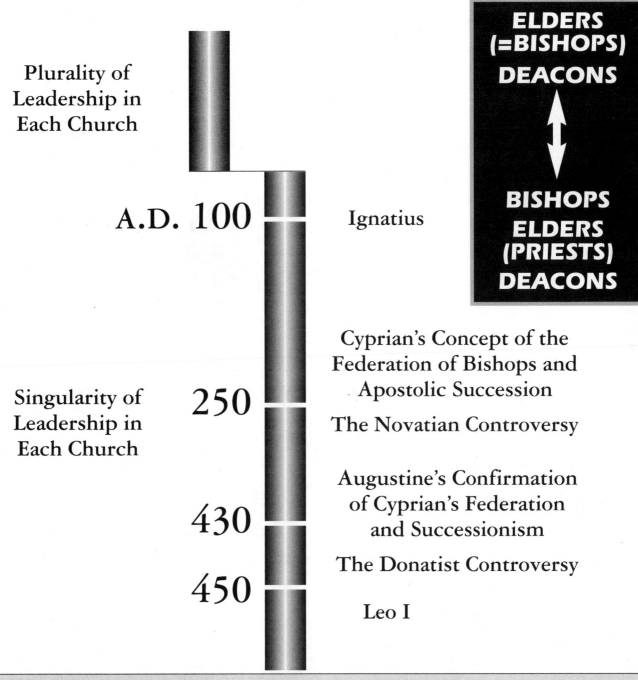

Plurality of Leadership in Each Church

ELDERS (=BISHOPS) DEACONS

↕

BISHOPS ELDERS (PRIESTS) DEACONS

A.D. 100 — Ignatius

Cyprian's Concept of the Federation of Bishops and Apostolic Succession

Singularity of Leadership in Each Church

250

The Novatian Controversy

Augustine's Confirmation of Cyprian's Federation and Successionism

430

The Donatist Controversy

450

Leo I

As the number of believers multiplied, the way the churches were directed changed. The New Testament pattern was one of a plurality of leadership in the churches. There were elders (also called bishops and overseers) and deacons. By the end of the first century a trend was discernible that would be the norm for several centuries. The terms *elders* and *bishops* came to signify separate offices. Elders remained a plurality in the churches; bishops did not. Thus, in each church a pattern developed of having a single bishop over each church—a quasi-episcopal form of government. No bishop, however, was seen as having a greater apostolic authority than any others throughout the empire.

Chart 25

The Concept of Authority in the Early Church

GOD

CHRIST

APOSTLES

THE APOSTLES' SUCCESSORS

A succession of bishops from God through Christ in the churches

A single apostolic successor in each church (that is, a bishop)

An emphasis on a linearly passed, entrusted tradition

The early church possessed the Old Testament Scriptures and viewed them as anticipatory of the greater revelation of Christ. Since the New Testament writings were emerging in a noncohesive fashion and were not universally recognized, the question of the authority of the message was paramount. "How do you know this new message is true?" the early churchmen were frequently asked. The reply of the early church was that of a *truth succession* (an oral tradition of the gospel). God revealed his word through and in Christ, Christ conveyed that message to the apostles, who in turn taught it to their successors, the bishops in the churches. Authority resided in the church through the bishop, who was a successor of an apostle.

Chart 26

The Components of Early Church Government

Monarchical Bishop **+** Apostolic Succession **=** Episcopal Ecclesiology

Ignatius of Antioch   Clement of Rome

The ideas of a single bishop in each church (a view seen earliest in Ignatius of Antioch) and a succession of bishops stemming from an apostle (a view seen earliest in Clement of Rome) are related to the issue of the authority of the new message of the gospel and the Christian faith. The shift to a single bishop was only gradually achieved; for example, plurality of leadership in the church at Rome continued into the time of bishop Sixtus in the second century.

Chart 27

The Earliest Church Fathers and End-Time Events

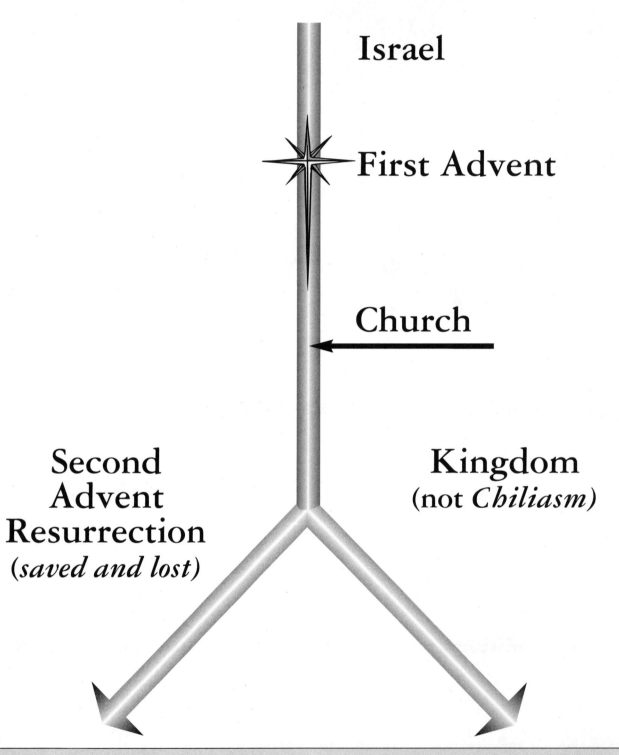

Israel

First Advent

Church

Second
Advent
Resurrection
(*saved and lost*)

Kingdom
(not *Chiliasm*)

The earliest church fathers held to a firm hope of Christ's return. However difficult the times, the world was to end with the triumph of God over his enemies. These writers seemed to have embraced an embryonic form of premillennialism, believing that Christ would return to earth to reign as king. After the "millennium," there was to be a great judgment of all mankind.

Chart 28

The Age of the
Apologists
(from 150 to 300)

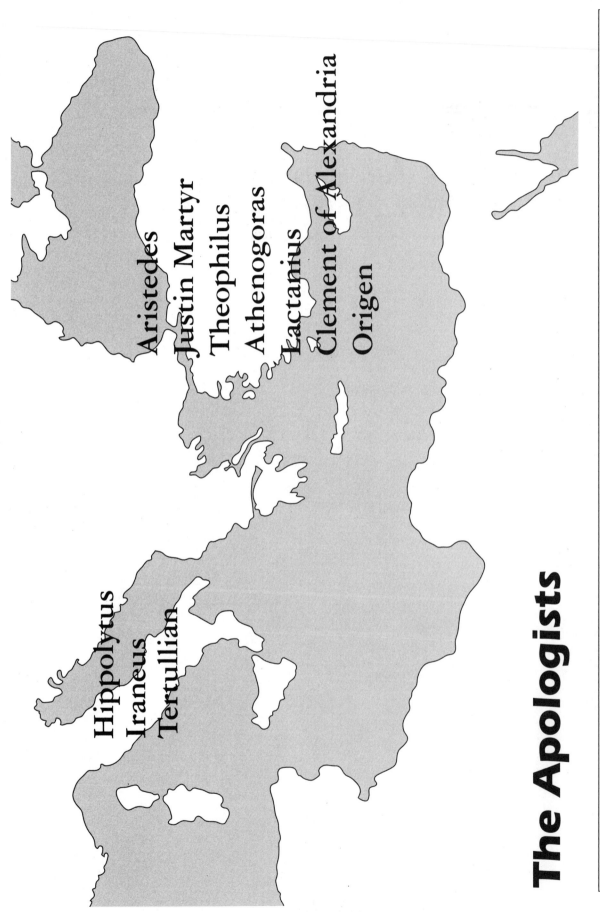

Aristedes
Justin Martyr
Theophilus
Athenogoras
Lactanius
Clement of Alexandria
Origen

Hippolytus
Iraneus
Tertullian

The Apologists

The apologists were second-century writers who contended for the faith, answering the accusations of critics from inside (Marcion, for example) and outside the church (Celsus, for example). The polemical nature of their writings marks their time as a distinct era in the history of the church. Most of the writers were from the Eastern portion of the church.

Chart 29

Callslip Request   12/16/2013 3:24:23 PM

Request date: 12/13/2013 04:32 PM
Request ID: 43163
Call Number: 270.0202 H2436
Item Barcode:

3 4 7 1 1 0 0 1 5 8 1 9 2 7

Author: Hannah, John D.
Title: Charts of ancient and medieval church h
Enumeration: c.1 Year:
Patron Name: Joseph Franks
Patron Barcode:

6 0 6 0 7 3

Patron comment:

Request number:

Route to:

4 3 1 6 3

I-Share Library:

Library Pick Up Location:

Early Church Writers and Writings

Writings	Events	Church Leaders and Writers
	Jesus' crucifixion and resurrection	
Paul's Letters		Council of Jerusalem
	Paul's Missionary Journeys	
Josephus's History	Fall of Jerusalem	
Didache	Eruption of Vesuvius	Clement of Rome
Ignatius's Letters		Justin Martyr
Justin's *Apology*	Marcion excommunicated	Tertullian
Irenaeus's *Against Heresies*	Montanism starts in Phrygia	Irenaeus Origen Cyprian
Tertullian's *Apology*		
Origen's *Against Celsus*	Novatianists set up congregation in Rome	Antony
	Empire divides East/West	

0
25
50
75
100
125
150
175
200
225
250
275
300

Chart 30

Emperors and Persecutions

	Roman Emperors	Events	Christians Persecuted
0	Tiberius		
25	Claudius	Council of Jerusalem	
50	Nero	Fall of Jerusalem	Rome
75	Vespasian / Titus	Eruption of Vesuvius	Asia
100	Trajan / Hadrian		
125			
150	Antonius Pius / Marcus	Marcion excommunicated	Polycarp / Rome, Gaul, and Africa
175	Aurelius	Montanism starts in Phrygia	
200	Septimus Severus		
225			
	Decius	Novatianists set up congregation in Rome	Decian Persecution
250	Valerian / Gallienus		
275		Empire divides East/West	
300	Diocletian		Diocletian Persecution

Chart 31

The Schools of Thought in Early Christianity

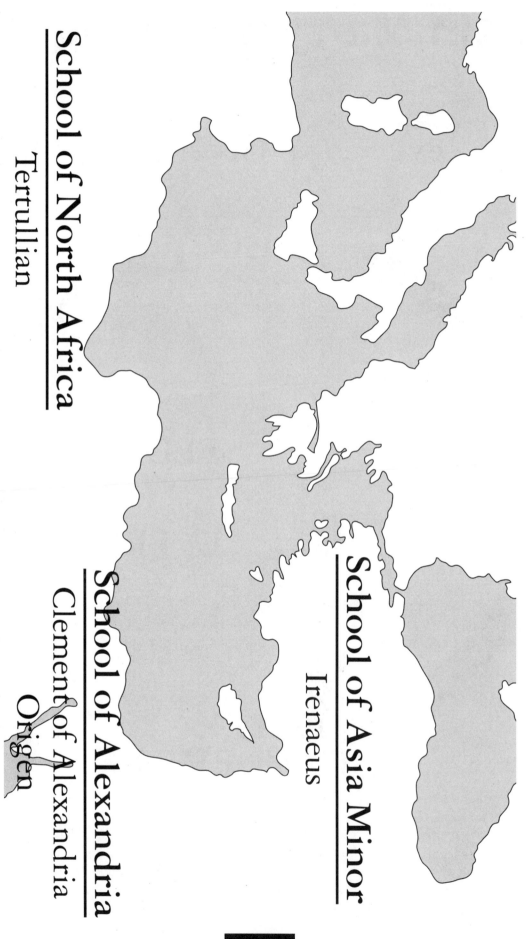

School of Asia Minor
Irenaeus

School of Alexandria
Clement of Alexandria
Origen

School of North Africa
Tertullian

Several distinct schools of thought emerged in the second century in the defense and explanation of the Christian faith. The school of Alexandria championed the faith by using a strong philosophical, spiritualizing tendency in its approach to Scripture. The school of Asia Minor stressed a grammatical and historical approach. The school of North Africa emphasized reason and authority.

Chart 32

Justin Martyr's Apologetics

Truth Revealed to Greek Philosophers

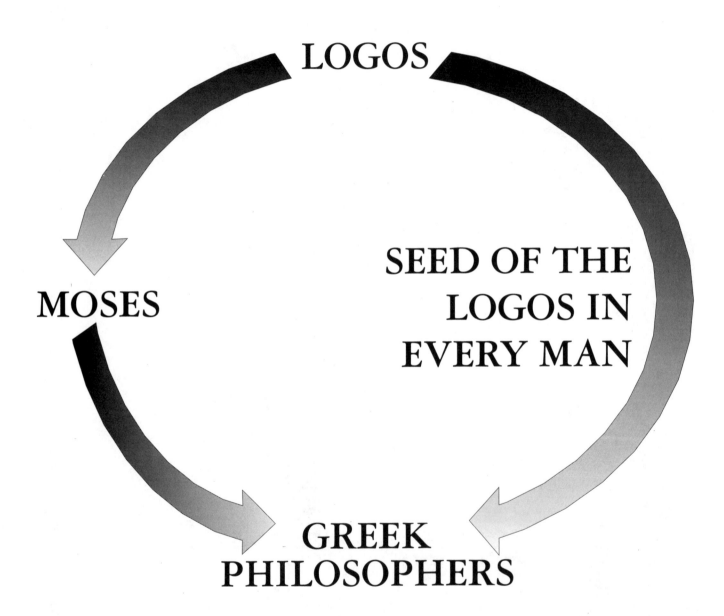

LOGOS

SEED OF THE LOGOS IN EVERY MAN

MOSES

GREEK PHILOSOPHERS

One of the earliest approaches to the defense of the Christian faith is seen in Justin Martyr's writings. In his argument against paganism, he stated that the Greek philosophers were correct in some matters because they possessed the Spirit of Christ without knowing it (though they did so partially). Moses most fully revealed Christ, so that if anyone wanted to be a true follower of the truth, they should embrace the Old Testament Scriptures, which spoke of the coming Christ.

Chart 33

Clement of Alexandria

on Philosophy

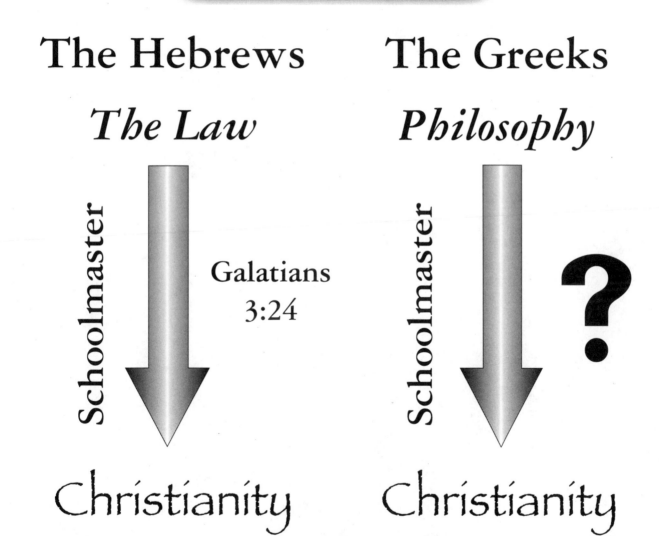

The Hebrews

The Law

Schoolmaster

Galatians 3:24

Christianity

The Greeks

Philosophy

Schoolmaster

?

Christianity

Clement of Alexandria formulated a defense of the Christian faith in a slightly different way from Justin Martyr. He suggested that the Old Testament, the Law, was given to the Jews to lead them to Christ. Similarly, God gave philosophy to the Greeks, which, when properly understood, should have the same result for them as the Law did for Jews. To be a true philosopher is to be led through philosophy to Christ.

Chart 34

Clement of Alexandria
on Levels of Christian Experience

"Gnostic"
Higher Knowledge

Simple Believer
Faith

Clement and the school of Alexandria championed a concept of gradations of spiritual knowledge based on spiritual maturation. For the "normal" believer, the Bible is to be approached with childlike faith and accepted for its literal meaning. For the more experienced Christian, a richer, more spiritual meaning lies below the surface of the texts.

Chart 35

The Apologists and Their Understanding of Christ

| Agent of Creation | Agent of Revelation | Incarnate Son of God |

The apologists struggled to explain the relationship of the Father to the Son because they lacked the technical vocabulary and insight of subsequent writers. While none stated that Christ was less than God, they generally referred to him as God's agent and servant, thus suggesting something less than the absolute equality of the Father and the Son.

Chart 36

Irenaeus and the Recapitulation Theory of the Atonement

Adam

First Man

Law Broken

Lost Eternal
Life for Man

Christ

Second Man

Law Obeyed

Regained for Man
What Adam Lost

While Irenaeus, perhaps the greatest churchman until Athanasius, did not seek to explain the meaning of Christ's death, he laid the basic framework for later discussions. He explained the accomplishments of Christ's death by emphasizing the benefits that Christ procured. This view is often called reinstitutionalism or recapitulation and is derived from the "first Adam–second Adam" analogy of Romans 5:12–21. As Adam broke the law, thereby plunging humanity into ruin, Christ obeyed the law, thereby regaining what Adam lost for the race, namely, spiritual life.

Chart 37

Origen and the Ransom-to-Satan View of the Atonement

PAYMENT

BONDAGE

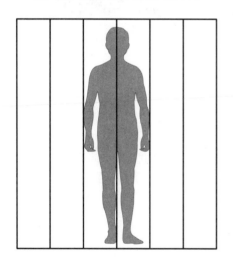

RELEASE

CHRIST'S RIGHTEOUSNESS

Though Origen's understanding of Christ's death is hampered by contradictory statements, scholars have generally assumed that he taught a concept of the atonement called "Ransom to Satan." Origen viewed humans as being under divine judgment and in bondage to the devil. Christ was the only one who could make the required payment for the sinner's release from bondage. It seems, though, that he viewed Christ's death as a payment made to the devil, overlooking the Bible's notion that we are in bondage to the devil because we are indebted *to God*. The release of the sinner was not to be gained by a payment to Satan, but by a payment to God so as to preserve his justice when justifying sinners.

Chart 38

Baptism in the Early Church

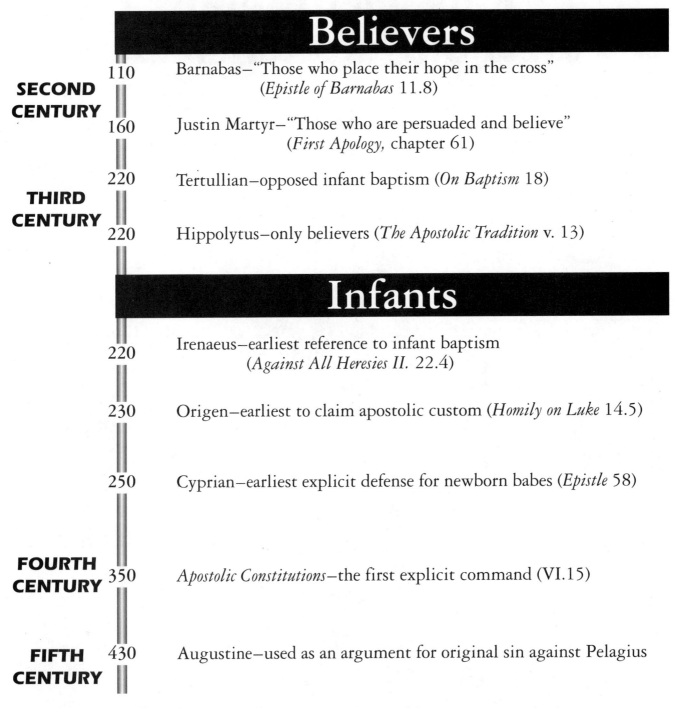

Believers

SECOND CENTURY

110   Barnabas–"Those who place their hope in the cross"
      (*Epistle of Barnabas* 11.8)

160   Justin Martyr–"Those who are persuaded and believe"
      (*First Apology,* chapter 61)

THIRD CENTURY

220   Tertullian–opposed infant baptism (*On Baptism* 18)

220   Hippolytus–only believers (*The Apostolic Tradition* v. 13)

Infants

220   Irenaeus–earliest reference to infant baptism
      (*Against All Heresies* II. 22.4)

230   Origen–earliest to claim apostolic custom (*Homily on Luke* 14.5)

250   Cyprian–earliest explicit defense for newborn babes (*Epistle* 58)

FOURTH CENTURY

350   *Apostolic Constitutions*–the first explicit command (VI.15)

FIFTH CENTURY

430   Augustine–used as an argument for original sin against Pelagius

Infant baptism is by this time a general practice

Baptism, along with the Lord's Supper, were the sacraments of the early church. In the first and second centuries baptism was restricted to believers. References to infant baptism first appeared in the third century. In the early church baptism was extended only to those who intellectually understood and affirmed the faith. *Infant baptism* does not suggest a particular age of a person and does not necessarily refer to those incapable of learning. Thus, infants were baptized in the early church, but we have no indication that they were newborns.

Chart 39

Baptism and Salvation in the Early Church

> "He saved us through the washing of rebirth and renewal by the Holy Spirit." Titus 3:5

3 - YEAR PROCESS

Private Instruction	
"Hearer"	Allowed to attend the ministry of the Word
"Kneeler"	Allowed to stay after the ministry of the Word for prayer
Examination by bishop and preparation for baptism	Water and spiritual baptism
	Regeneration (conversion)
	church member
	Eucharist
Spiritual rebirth **SAVED**	Hippolytus, *The Apostolic Tradition*

While it seems unorthodox to many Protestants, the early church viewed salvation as occurring at the same time as water baptism. Those interested in the Christian faith were designated as learners or disciples. The instruction period lasted a number of years, with each disciple progressing in knowledge and experience. After a period of time, they would prepare for baptism. Coming to the water as believers, these persons would confess their faith in Christ and be washed with physical water and seen as washed by the Spirit with spiritual life. Afterward they were welcomed into the community and participation in its most sacred ritual, the Lord's Supper.

Chart 40

The Lord's Supper in the Early Church

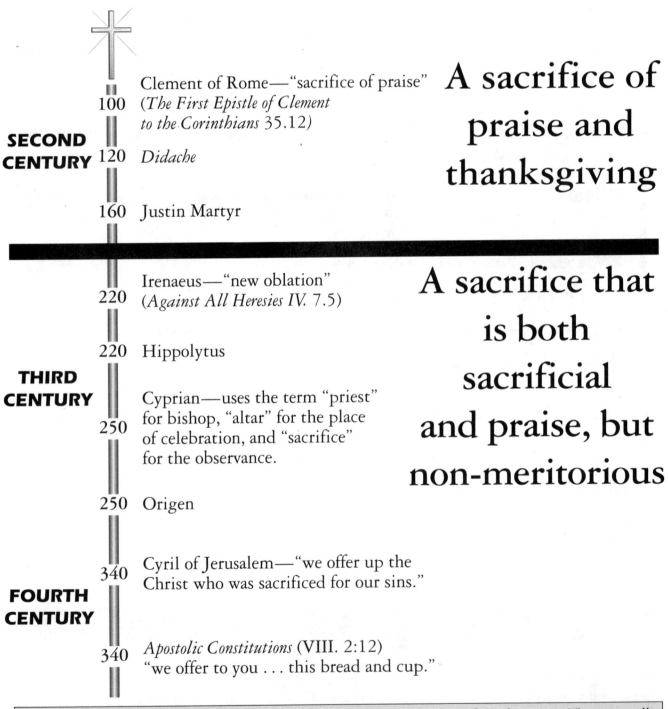

SECOND CENTURY

100 Clement of Rome—"sacrifice of praise" (*The First Epistle of Clement to the Corinthians* 35.12)

120 *Didache*

160 Justin Martyr

A sacrifice of praise and thanksgiving

THIRD CENTURY

220 Irenaeus—"new oblation" (*Against All Heresies IV.* 7.5)

220 Hippolytus

250 Cyprian—uses the term "priest" for bishop, "altar" for the place of celebration, and "sacrifice" for the observance.

250 Origen

A sacrifice that is both sacrificial and praise, but non-meritorious

FOURTH CENTURY

340 Cyril of Jerusalem—"we offer up the Christ who was sacrificed for our sins."

340 *Apostolic Constitutions* (VIII. 2:12) "we offer to you . . . this bread and cup."

The writers in the early church viewed the Lord's Supper as a celebration of thanksgiving. They generally believed Christ to be present in the bread and wine, though with none of the sacramentalism and merit-deriving language that would characterize late medieval interpretations. The churchmen used Old Testament terminology and spoke of the Lord's Supper as a sacrifice, of the place of offering as the altar, and of themselves as priests.

Chart 41

The Apologists
and End-Time Events

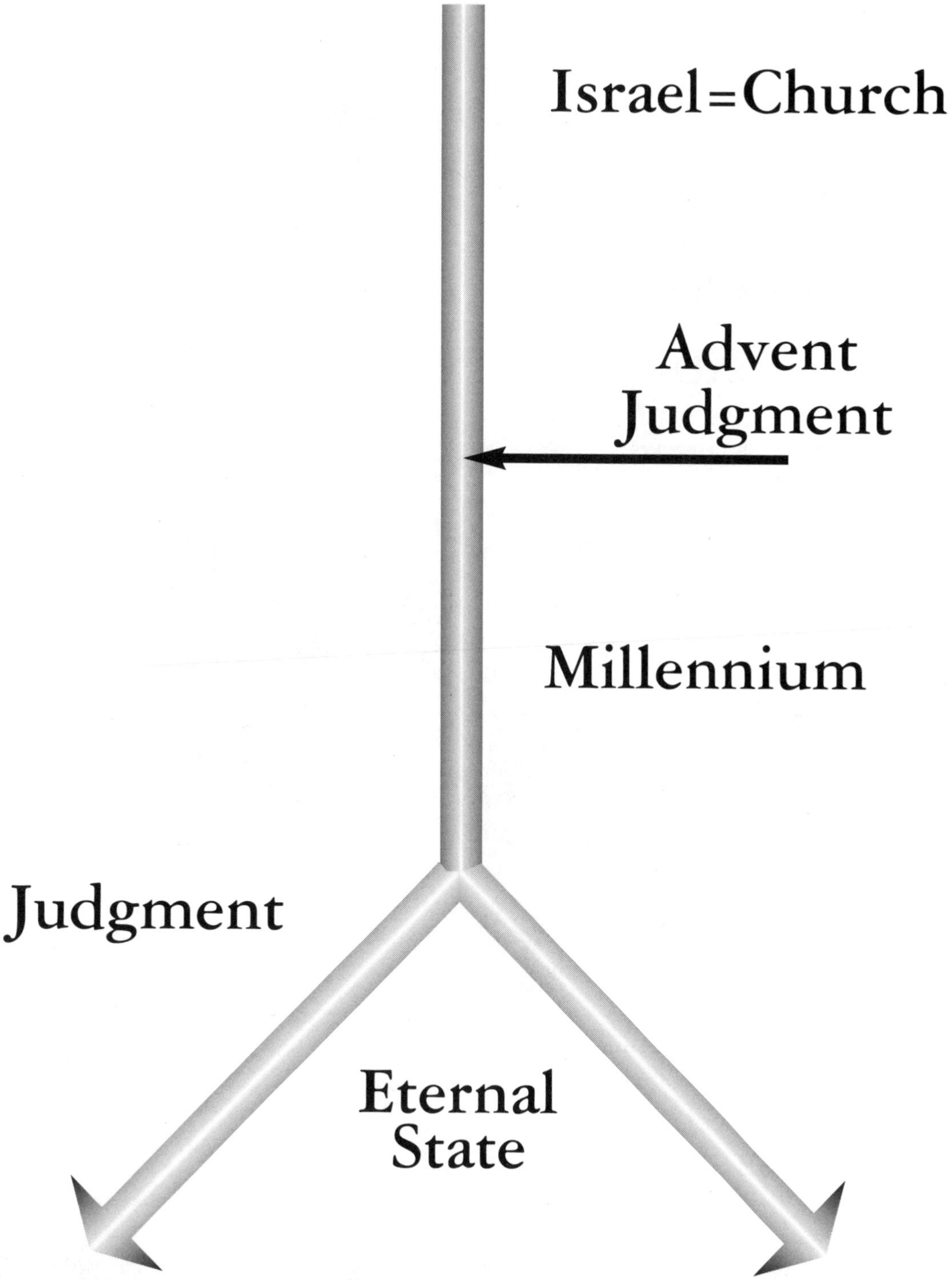

Israel=Church

Advent
Judgment

Millennium

Judgment

Eternal
State

Evident in the writings of Justin Martyr, Irenaeus, and Tertullian was a premillennial understanding of end-time events. They envisioned Christ returning to the earth to visibly reign from Jerusalem for a thousand years, followed by the great judgment and the eternal state. In contrast to later forms of premillennialism, they conceived of Israel and the church as one.

Chart 42

Gnosticism: Perplexing Questions

How can the existence of creation be explained?

What is the origin of evil?

How can a holy God create a universe with sin?

The Christian faith was opposed by numerous adversaries—threats from the state, ominous false religions, and heretics within its own borders. The most imposing religious threat came from Gnosticism, which was particularly dangerous because of its intellectual coherency. While Gnosticism seemed to provide answers to perplexing questions, it succeeded only in mixing a snippet of biblical truth with error.

Chart 43

Essential Components of Gnosticism

Dualism

Emanations

Knowledge

God
(Pure Spirit)

Demiurge

World

Man

Gnosticism taught (1) that there is a radical dualism of the spiritual in opposition to the material (God, who is Spirit, is the supreme good, while matter is evil); (2) that God could not have created matter because it is contrary to his nature; rather, the world, which is material and evil, was created by the Demiurge (an emanation from God), and man is a material being with an entrapped spirit; and (3) that through a "secret knowledge," salvation becomes the life of escape from the material confines of the body.

Chart 44

Gnosticism's Concept of Salvation

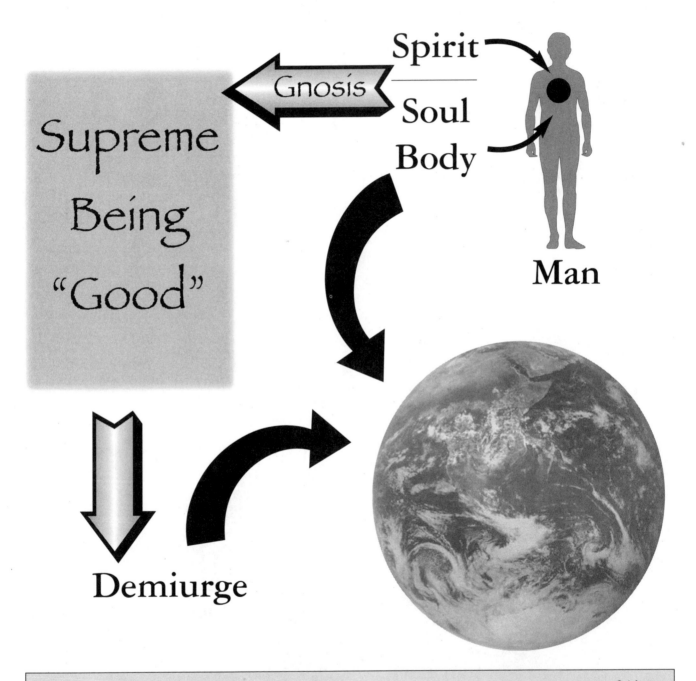

Gnosticism's concept of salvation is as follows: God did not create the world, but a lesser yet powerful being (the Demiurge) made this evil world and mankind—though within man is a spark of good. Salvation results from enlarging the capacity of that nature while minimizing the hold of materialism, and it is accomplished by means of the secret teachings of Gnostic teachers. In resisting this teaching, Christian writers adopted a worldview that embraced the God of the Bible as the divine creator, affirmed the creation as good though marred by a subsequent devastation, and espoused the salvation of the body as well as the soul.

Chart 45

Manicheanism

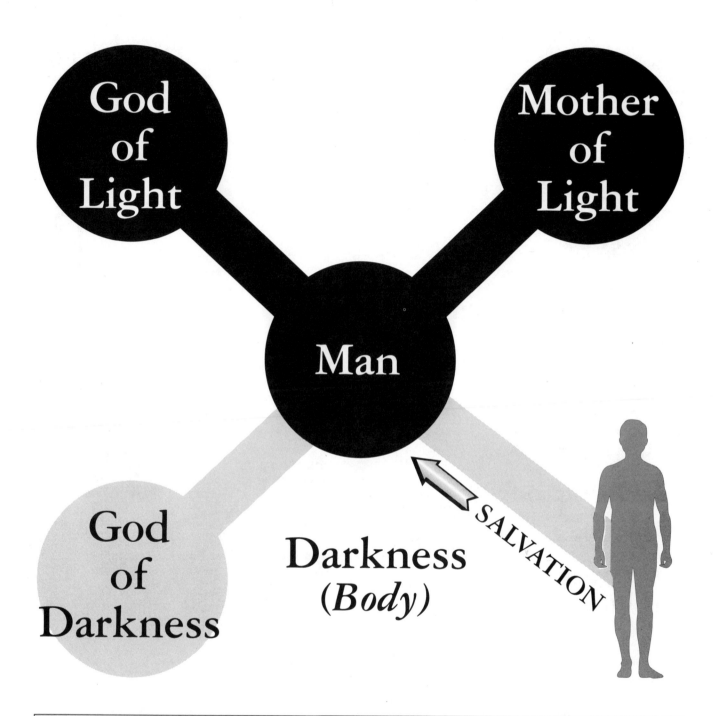

God
of
Light

Mother
of
Light

Man

God
of
Darkness

Darkness
(*Body*)

SALVATION

The Manichean heresy posed another threat from outside the church. Like the Gnostics, the Manicheans embraced the notion of a spiritual/material dualism. Once a spirit, humans were tricked by the god of darkness (a material being) and plunged into the confines of a physical body. Salvation from the physical appetites is gained through following Manichean formulas and rigorous ascetic practices. Augustine once embraced Manichean teaching, but found his physical appetites to be too great to be overcome by mental denial. The solution was not in denying his fallen humanity but in counting himself as having died with Christ to sin's ruling power.

Chart 46

Marcionism

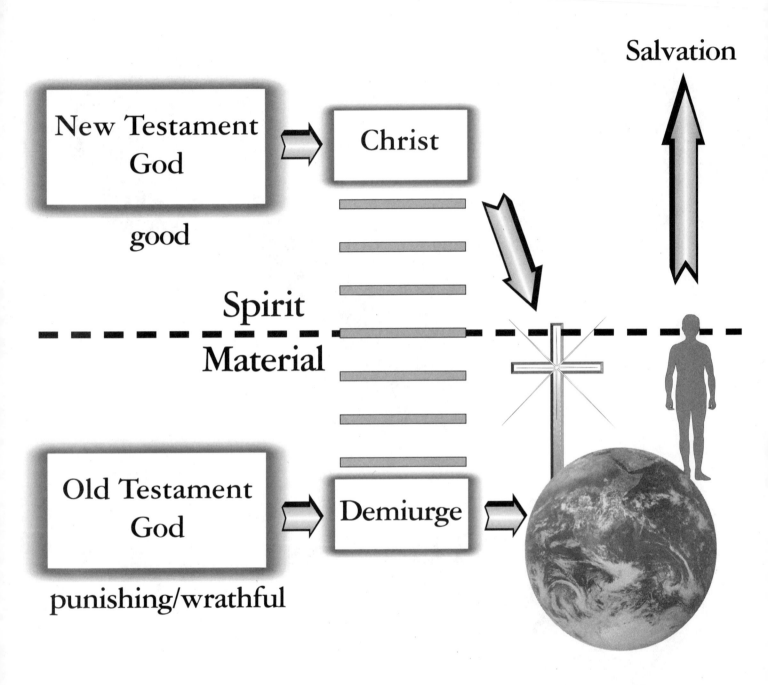

Marcionism was a second-century Christian sect that separated from the church by 144. Marcion embraced certain tenets of Gnosticism, blending them with a critical approach to Christian teachings. He adopted a radical dualism (spirit and matter) and viewed the New Testament God as spiritual but the Old Testament God as material. Christ was good, but only spiritual; the Demiurge was evil, yet the creator of everything material. Christ came to redeem us, but only in the appearance of the flesh, and the Demiurge fought against him to kill him. Because Christ was spirit, not flesh, he could not be defeated and so rose from the *appearance* of death and is the way of salvation. In response to Marcionism, Christian writers argued that Christ was truly human and that he truly died and rose from the dead. Creator and redeemer are one and the same person.

Chart 47

Gnosticism and Marcionism Compared

Gnosticism	Marcionism
O.T.: reinterpret spiritually, embraced it	O.T.: interpret literally, but rejected it
N.T.: make additions (Gospel of Thomas)	N.T.: eliminate unwanted material
Secret knowledge	No secret knowledge (careful study of Paul)
Highly speculative	No interest in speculation
Founded schools	Founded churches

Gnostics and Marcionites had remarkable affinities as well as distinct differences. Gnostics dealt with the troublesome elements in the Old Testament by spiritualizing them; Marcionites rejected these elements as noncanonical. Marcionites eliminated from the New Testament any material contrary to their teachings; Gnostics added books that supported their views. Marcionites advocated the teachings of the apostle Paul but said there were no Jewish elements in the New Testament.

Chart 48

Montanism

Tongues
Revelation
Healing

Originating from Asia Minor in the second century, Montanism was restorationist by intent. Montanists (Tertullian was probably its best-known adherent) believed that the church had become morally weak. It was a rigorist sect that called the church back to a former, better day. They emphasized the renewal of such neglected spiritual gifts as healing and tongue speaking. Because some Montanists advocated continued revelation, the movement was viewed as dangerous by the church's leadership. Montanism did have a positive influence by forcing the church to clarify issues of the canon (as did Marcionism) and the role of extraordinary spiritual gifts.

Chart 49

Church-State Relations

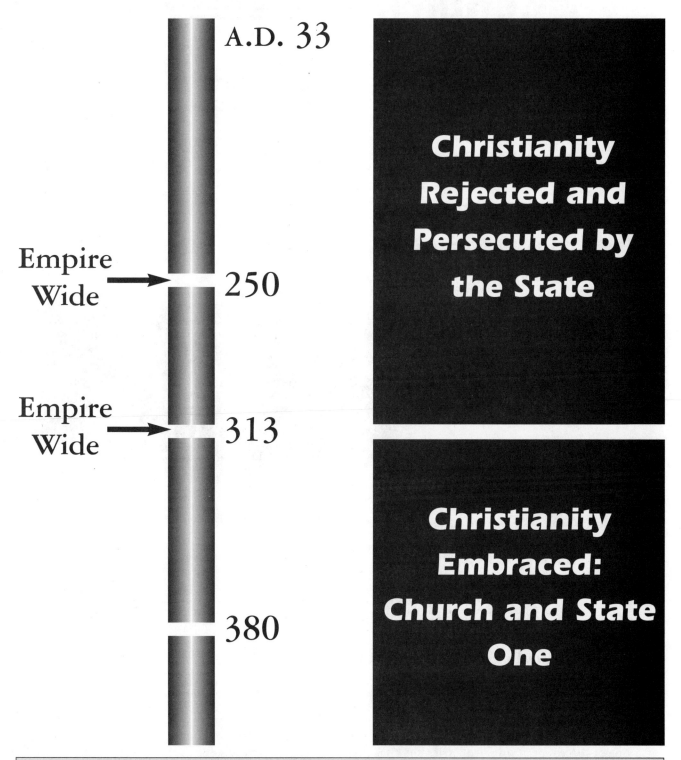

A.D. 33

Empire Wide → 250

Empire Wide → 313

380

Christianity Rejected and Persecuted by the State

Christianity Embraced: Church and State One

The relationship of Christianity to the Roman Empire was contentious. While the Romans worshiped a pantheon of deities, the refusal of Christians to worship anything other than the one true God posed a problem for Rome. Persecution of Christians was generally sporadic, though they enjoyed no official status until the time of Constantine. Twice the church experienced empire-wide persecution (during the reigns of emperors Decius and Diocletian). With Constantine came the toleration of Christianity and with Theodosius I its triumph.

Chart 50

The Response of the Ancient Church to Heresy

Doctrine of Apostolic Succession

Development of the Roman Creed

Development of the New Testament Canon

The church responded to the inroads of heretical teachings by (1) supporting the claim that the bishops stood in a line of succession from the apostles and that their teachings were the same as the apostles' teachings, (2) creating confessions of faith that would eventually lead to early creeds such as the Apostles' Creed, and (3) formally gathering together the books of the New Testament and recognizing an authoritative list of books to be read in the churches (in the realization that the church needed more than the doctrine of apostolic succession to ward off the heretics, since they also claimed to be apostolic and to possess what they claimed were holy writings).

Chart 51

The Old Roman Symbol: A Baptismal Confession

I believe in God the Father Almighty (*pantokratora*): and in Christ Jesus His only-begotten Son, our Lord, who was born of the Holy Spirit and the Virgin Mary, who under Pontius Pilate was crucified and buried, in the third day rose from the dead, ascended unto the heavens, and sat at the right hand of the Father, from whence He shall come to judge the living and the dead; and in the Holy Spirit, the holy Church, the remission of sins, and the resurrection of the flesh.

The Old Roman Symbol, dating from the middle of the second century, is one of Christianity's earliest confessions and is the forerunner of the Apostles' Creed. Its anti-gnostic nature made it a significant statement of orthodoxy.

Chart 52

The Major Bishoprics in the Roman Empire

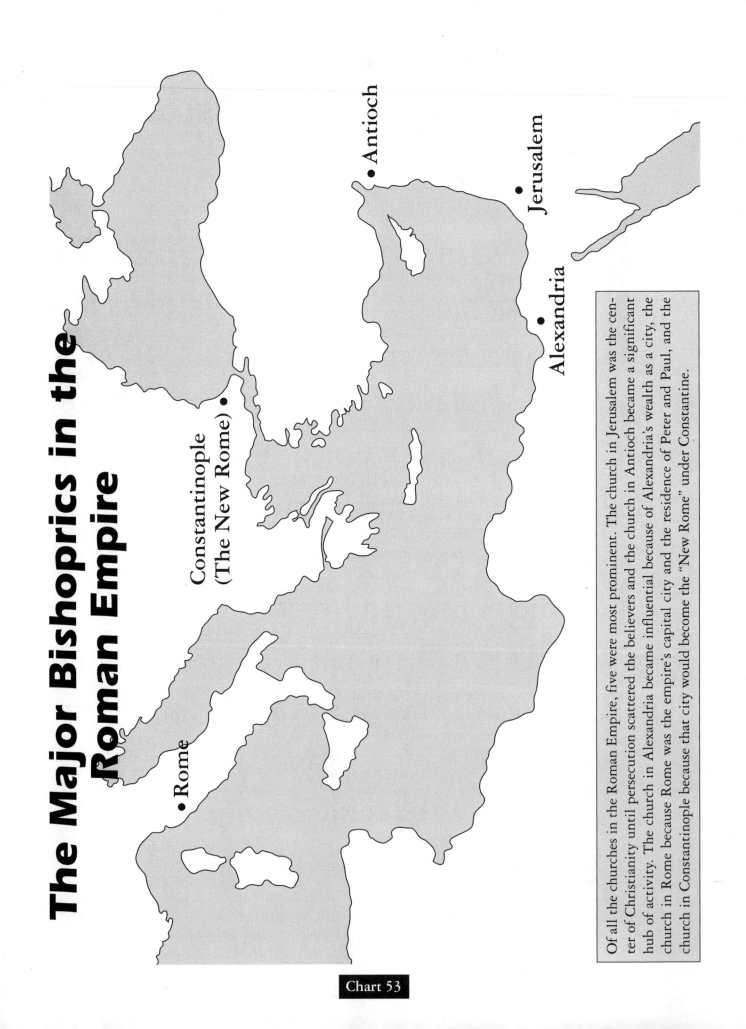

Antioch

Jerusalem

Alexandria

Constantinople
(The New Rome)

Rome

Of all the churches in the Roman Empire, five were most prominent. The church in Jerusalem was the center of Christianity until persecution scattered the believers and the church in Antioch became a significant hub of activity. The church in Alexandria became influential because of Alexandria's wealth as a city, the church in Rome because Rome was the empire's capital city and the residence of Peter and Paul, and the church in Constantinople because that city would become the "New Rome" under Constantine.

Chart 53

The Church in the Roman Empire

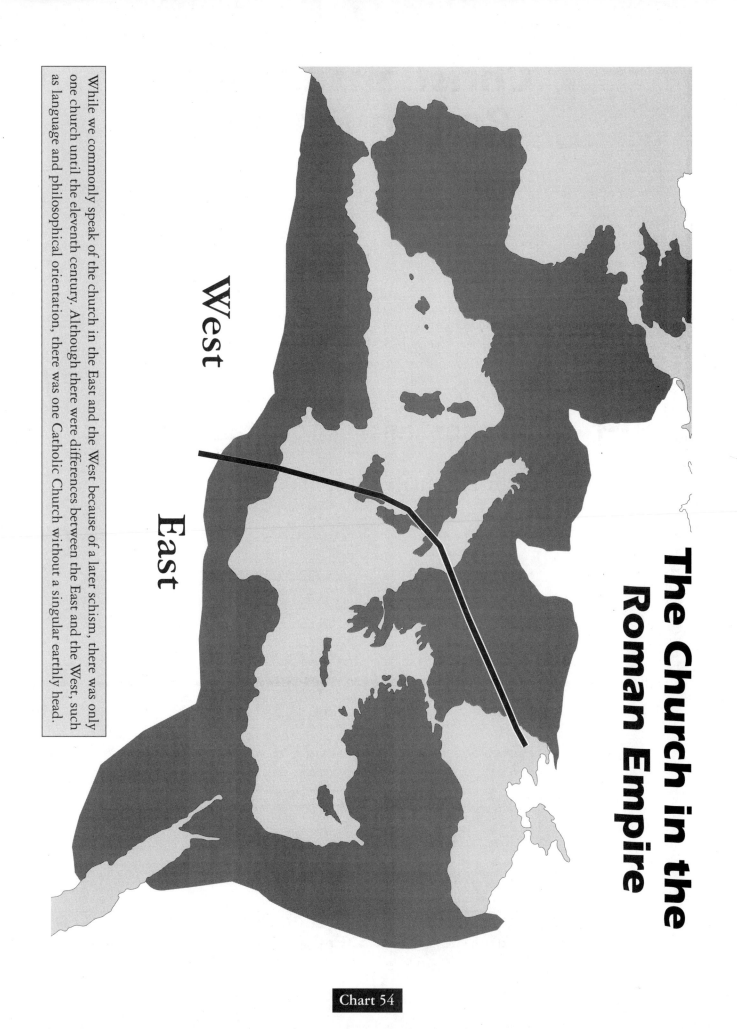

West

East

While we commonly speak of the church in the East and the West because of a later schism, there was only one church until the eleventh century. Although there were differences between the East and the West, such as language and philosophical orientation, there was one Catholic Church without a singular earthly head.

Chart 54

Christians in the Roman Empire

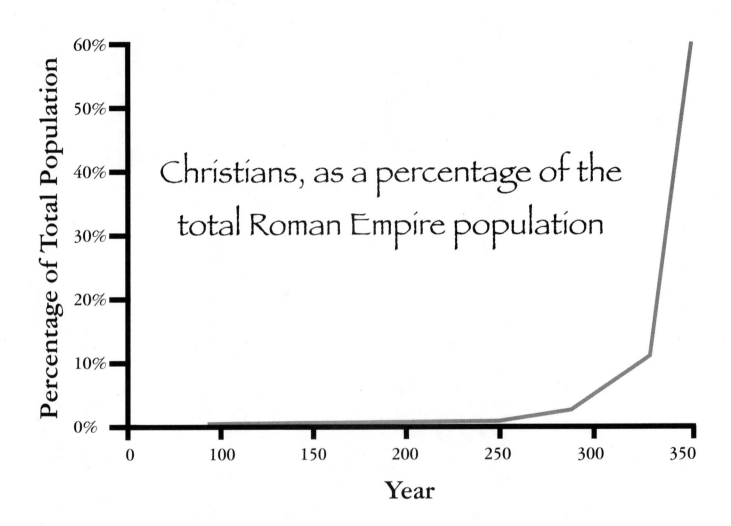

Christians, as a percentage of the total Roman Empire population

Christianity grew rapidly in the Roman Empire, particularly after Constantine established his toleration policy in the fourth century. By the middle of the century Christianity had become dominant and remained so for centuries.

Chart 55

The Triumph of the Church over the Empire
(from 300 to 600)

The Major Churchmen of the Period

300	10	20	30	40	**350**	60	70	80	90	**400**	10	20	30	40	**450**

ATHANASIUS OF ALEXANDRIA

Evagrius of Pontus

Basil of Caesarea

Gregory of Nazianzus

Gregory of Nyssa

Theodore of Mopsuestia

John Chrysostom

Synesius of Cyrene

Cyril of Alexandria

Theodoret of Cyrrhus

AUGUSTINE

Leo the Great

Prosper of Aquitaine

John Cassian

Paulinus of Nola

Jerome

Ambrose

Martin of Tours

Hilary of Poitiers

Caius Marius Victorinus

300	10	20	30	40	**350**	60	70	80	90	**400**	10	20	30	40	**450**

Two great churchmen dominated the era—Athanasius, the champion of the equality of the Father and the Son, and Augustine, the champion of the inability of man and the absolute necessity of the grace of God. It was a remarkable period in which the church broke the bonds of repression to dominate intellectual endeavor.

Chart 56

The Major Councils of the Early Church

NICAEA	325	ARIANISM
CONSTANTINOPLE	381	ARIANISM APOLLINARIANISM
EPHESUS	431	NESTORIANISM
CHALCEDON	451	EUTYCHIANISM
CONSTANTINOPLE	553	MONOPHYSITISM
CONSTANTINOPLE	680–681	MONOTHELETISM
NICAEA	787	ICONOCLASM

Because the church was emerging from persecution to a favored status, it became free for the first time to gather together, ironically at the behest of the emperors until the eleventh century, to address issues of concern. Seven major ecumenical councils took place, dealing with the issues of Christ's preincarnate relationship to the Father, the nature of Christ in the incarnation, and the place of icons in the church.

Chart 57

Adoptionism:
An Attempt to Explain Christ

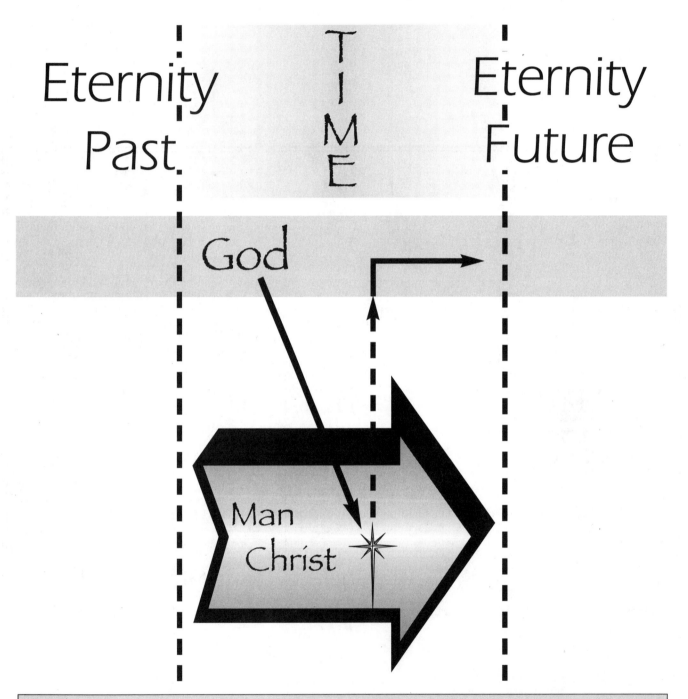

While the church firmly embraced the deity of Christ, churchmen found it difficult to explain the relationship of the Father to the Son. How can the church confess "the LORD our God, the LORD is one" and simultaneously affirm that Jesus Christ is God? *Adoptionism* was one attempt to explain the Father-Son relationship. Christ was a man on whom the power of God descended, and by adoption he became the Son of God. Later churchmen saw the peril in this explanation, which destroys the equality of Father and Son, making Christ less than the Father.

Chart 58

Modalism:
An Attempt to Explain Christ

Modalism was a difficult error to suppress in the church. Modalists argued that God is one—one being who appears in three forms. Modalists stressed the unity of God, an improvement over the Adoptionists, while denigrating the distinctiveness of persons in the Godhead.

Chart 59

Adoptionism and Modalism Compared

ADOPTIONISM
(Dynamic Modalism)

MODALISM
(Modalistic Monarchianism, Sabellianism, Patripassionism)

ADOPTIONISM	MODALISM
Stress Oneness of God	Stress Oneness of God
Deny Deity of Christ	Affirm Deity of Christ
Affirm Humanity of Christ	Deny Humanity of Christ
Holy Spirit = a power	Holy Spirit = a mode of God's existence

Adoptionism and Modalism both have strong points, yet each denies something essential to the Christian faith. Both affirm the singularity of God, but Adoptionism denies God's absolute deity and Modalism his humanity. In both explanations, the Holy Spirit is neglected.

Chart 60

Arianism

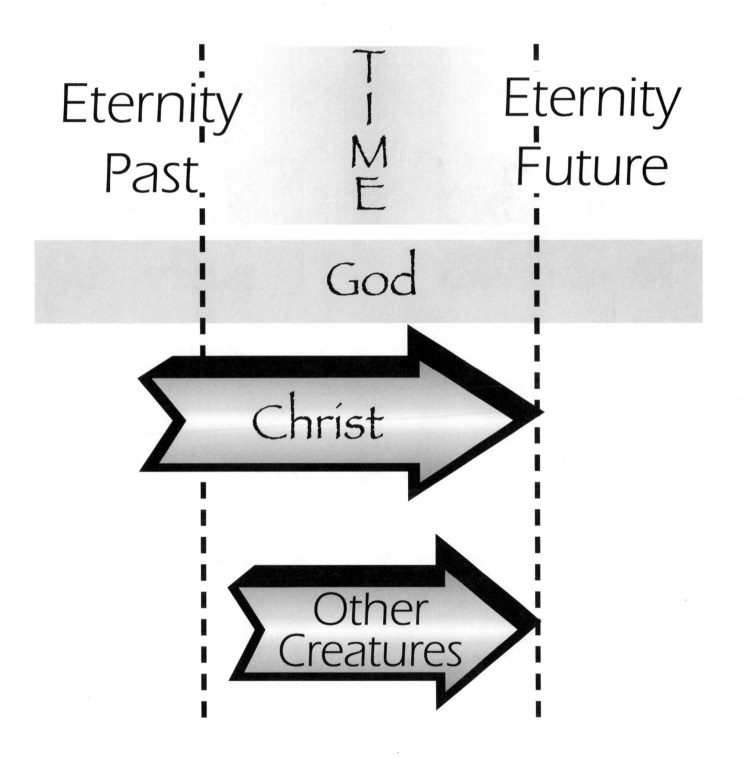

In the teachings of Arius, a presbyter in Alexandria, the issue of the Father-Son relationship came to a head. Arius argued that the dilemma of this relationship could be resolved by arguing that Christ was an eternally created being, that he was the firstborn of all things who, in turn, created all things. He was above all, yet not technically equal in every way with the Father.

Chart 61

Arianism:
The Opponents and the Issue

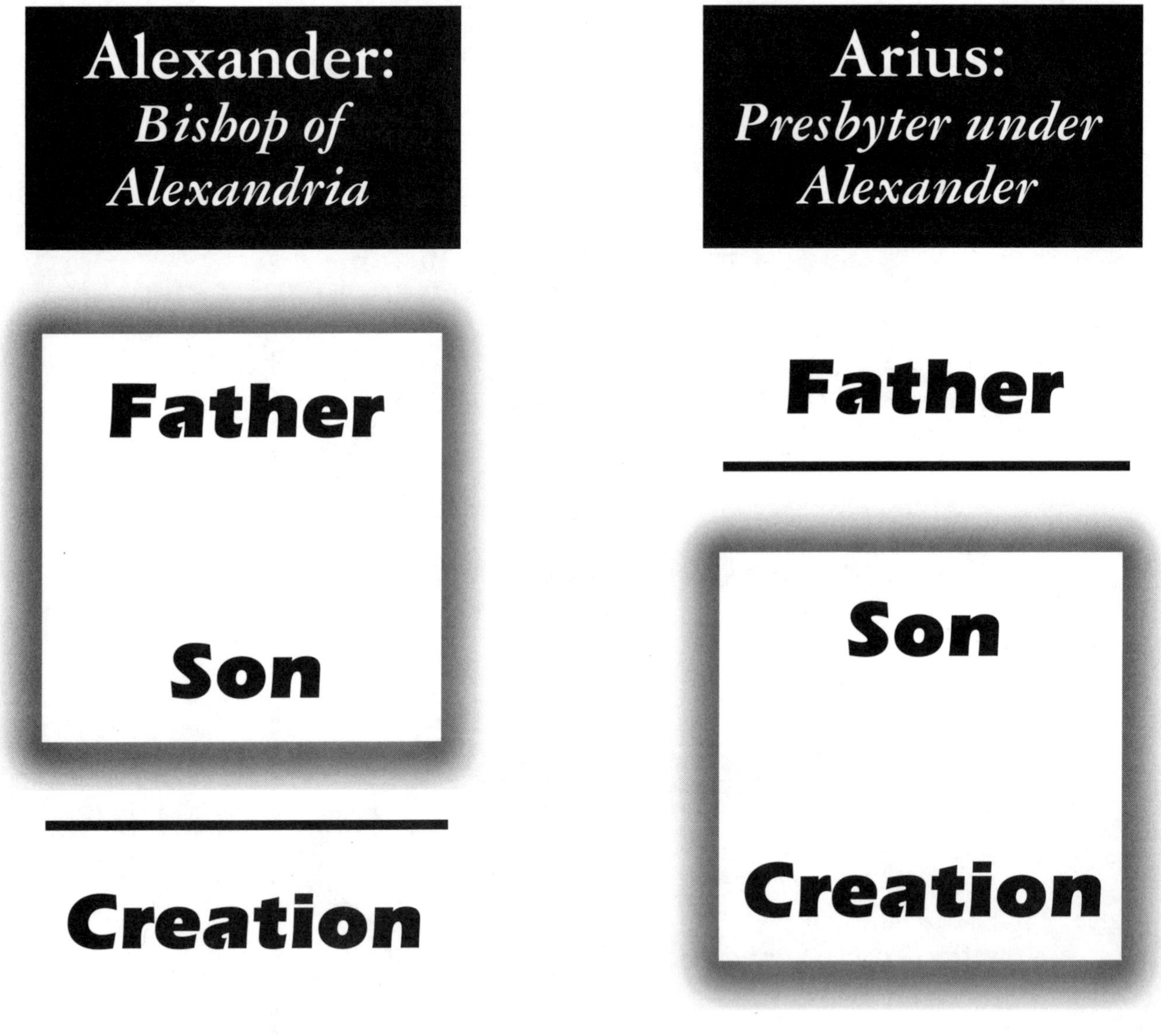

Alexander:
Bishop of Alexandria

Father

Son

Creation

Arius:
Presbyter under Alexander

Father

Son

Creation

Arius initially clashed with Alexander, bishop of Alexandria, and the issue became an empire-wide discussion. Alexander, and later more cogently Athanasius, argued that the Father and Son are truly one in the divine attributes. Arius subordinated the Son to the Father, contending that the Son was less than the Father in his proper nature.

Chart 62

The Nicene Creed (325)

We believe in one God, the Father All Governing, creator of all things visible and invisible;

And in one Lord Jesus Christ, the Son of God, begotten of the Father as only begotten, that is, from the essence [reality] of the Father, God from God, Light from Light, true God from true God, begotten not created, of the same essence [reality] as the Father, through whom all things came into being, both in heaven and in earth; Who for us men and for our salvation came down and was incarnate, becoming human. He suffered and the third day he rose, and ascended into the heavens. And he will come to judge both the living and the dead.

And [we believe] in the Holy Spirit.

Emperor Constantine called the bishops of the church to meet at Nicaea in 325. Churchmen affirmed the full equality of the Son with the Father and formulated the Nicene Creed. In the language of this creed, Christ was "begotten" of the Father but was "not created." He who had no beginning had a beginning, not of being, but of function through his "becoming human."

Chart 63

The Arian Controversy and Trinitarianism

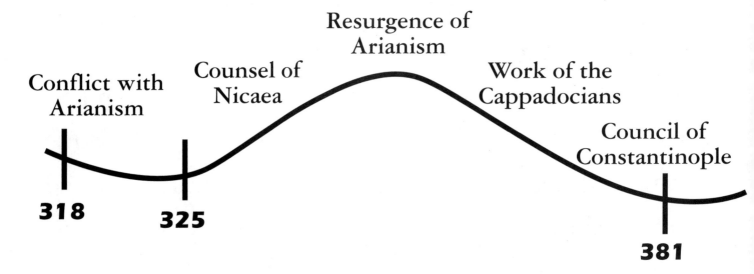

Resurgence of
Arianism

Counsel of
Nicaea

Conflict with
Arianism

Work of the
Cappadocians

Council of
Constantinople

318   **325**   **381**

Initial Rejection
of Arianism

Final Rejection
of Arianism

The Arian issue continued to trouble the church. The Eastern church feared that the wording of the creed was a concession to Modalism, which stressed the strict oneness of Father and Son. Western churchmen embraced the document as defending the equality of the persons in the Godhead. Through the writings of several influential churchmen and the extremes of the Arian party, the Council of Constantinople condemned Arianism in 381.

Chart 64

The Resurgence of Arianism

Resurgence of Arianism	Labor of Three Cappadocians
Arius versus Athanasius	Basil of Caesarea Gregory of Nyssa Gregory of Nazianzus
325 Council of Nicaea	**381 Council of Constantinople**

The writings of the three great Cappadocians from central Asia Minor sealed the doom of Arianism and the triumph of Athanasianism at the Council of Constantinople.

Chart 65

Trinitarianism
(*Error Avoided*)

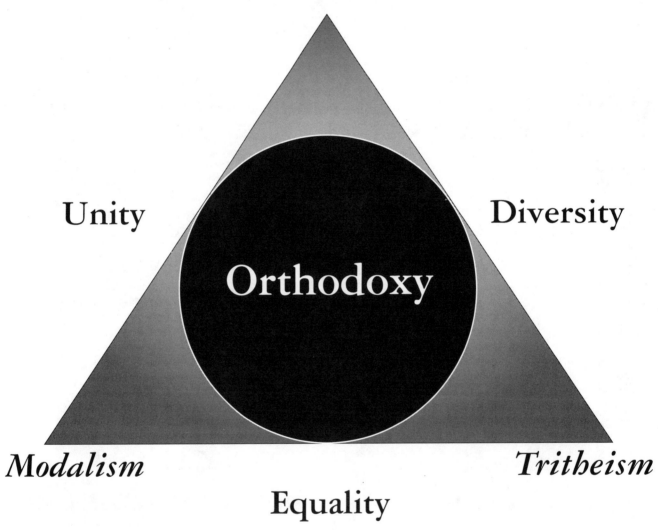

Subordination

Unity

Diversity

Orthodoxy

Modalism

Tritheism

Equality

The concept of the Trinity (the triunity of God) consists of three ideas: unity, diversity, and equality. God is one in characteristics (the attributes) and three in persons, and those three persons equally possess the same attributes. While confessing these truths, the church rejected Modalism (unity at the expense of diversity), Subordinationism (unity at the expense of equality), and Tritheism (plurality without singularity).

Chart 66

The Doctrine of God: Perspectives in the Christian Era

Competing Perspectives	A Singular Perspective	Competing Perspectives
Polytheism Dominant	Trinitarianism Dominant	No Consensus

325

1575

Council of Nicaea

"Era of the Triumph of Christianity"

Socinianism Unitarianism Deism

The doctrine of the triunity of God remained dominant in the church from Nicaea until the rise of the Socinians, Unitarians, and Deists in the sixteenth, seventeenth, and eighteenth centuries.

Chart 67

The Trinity and the Incarnate Christ Compared

	Unity	**Diversity**
TRINITY	Nature	Persons
CHRIST	Person	Natures

After the struggle to explain the mystery of the Trinity, the time came to clarify the issue of Christ's incarnate nature. How do we explain the relationship of his humanity to his deity when he was on earth? Before Christ came to earth, we confess his unity of being with the Father and the diversity of persons; in his incarnate state he was a single person possessing two perfect natures—human and divine.

Chart 68

The Major Schools of Thought in the Fourth-Century Christological Debates

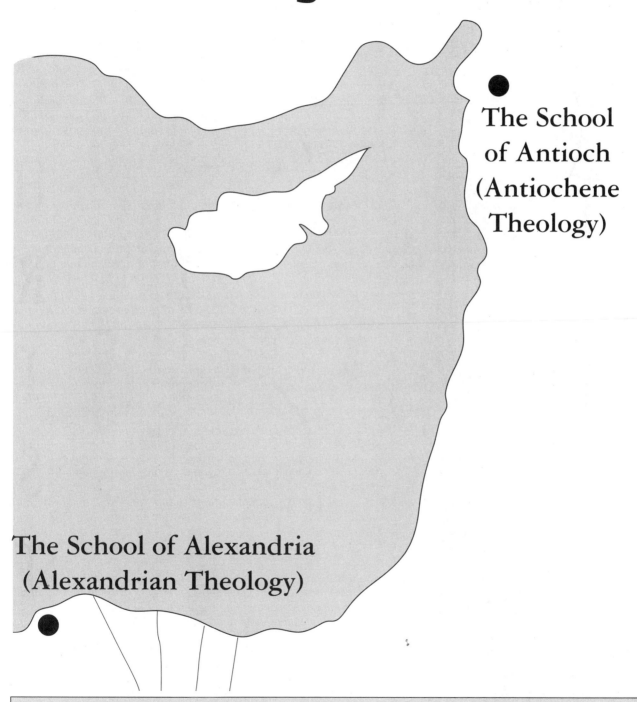

The School
of Antioch
(Antiochene
Theology)

The School of Alexandria
(Alexandrian Theology)

Two major schools of thought dominated the fourth century. The school of Antioch stressed the earthly life of Christ as described in the Gospels—his humanity. The school of Alexandria, greatly influenced by the struggle against Arianism, emphasized Christ's deity. Both were correct in what they affirmed, but their single-mindedness caused them to neglect the insights of the other. Christ is both truly God and truly man.

Chart 69

Apollinarianism
(A Denial of the Humanity of Christ)

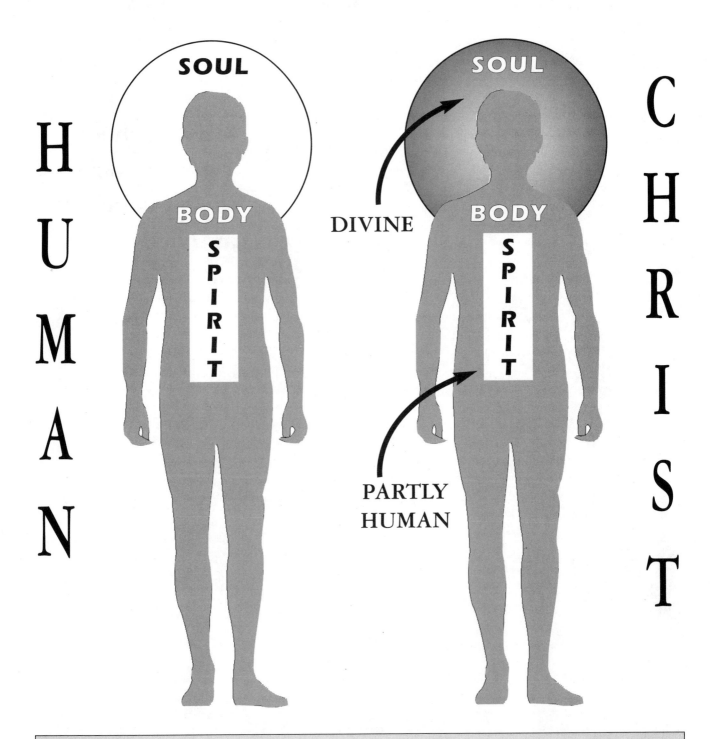

HUMAN

SOUL

BODY

SPIRIT

CHRIST

SOUL

DIVINE

BODY

SPIRIT

PARTLY HUMAN

The simmering controversy took tangible shape when the bishop of Laodicea, Apollinaris, affirmed Christ's deity but denigrated his humanity. His position was that Christ was truly God, but only partly man; he denied that Christ possessed a human spirit or mind.

Chart 70

The Creed of Constantinople (381)

We believe in one God, the Father All Governing [*pantokratora*], creator [*poieten*] of heaven and earth, of all things visible and invisible;

And in one Lord Jesus Christ, the only-begotten Son of God, begotten from the Father before all time [*pro panton ton aionon*], Light from Light, true God from true God, begotten not created [*poiethenta*], of the same essence [reality] as the Father [*homoousion to patri*], through Whom all things came into being, Who for us men and because of our salvation came down from heaven, and was incarnate by the Holy Spirit and the Virgin Mary and became human [*enanthropesanta*]. He was crucified for us under Pontius Pilate, and suffered and was buried, and rose on the third day, according to the Scriptures, and ascended to heaven, and sits on the right hand of the Father, and will come again with glory to judge the living and dead. His Kingdom shall have no end [*telos*].

And in the Holy Spirit, the Lord and life-giver, Who proceeds from the Father, Who is worshiped and glorified together with the Father and Son, Who spoke through the prophets; and in one, holy, catholic, and apostolic Church. We confess one baptism for the remission of sins. We look forward to the resurrection of the dead and the life of the world to come. Amen.

The second ecumenical council, held in Constantinople (381), condemned the teachings of Apollinaris and affirmed that Christ "became human." The cry of the churchmen was, "How could Christ heal what he did not possess?" If Christ was only partially human, the part he did not share with us could not be healed. Christ could not be our redeemer if he did not *fully* identify with us.

Chart 71

Nestorianism
(A Divided Christ: Denial of Unity)

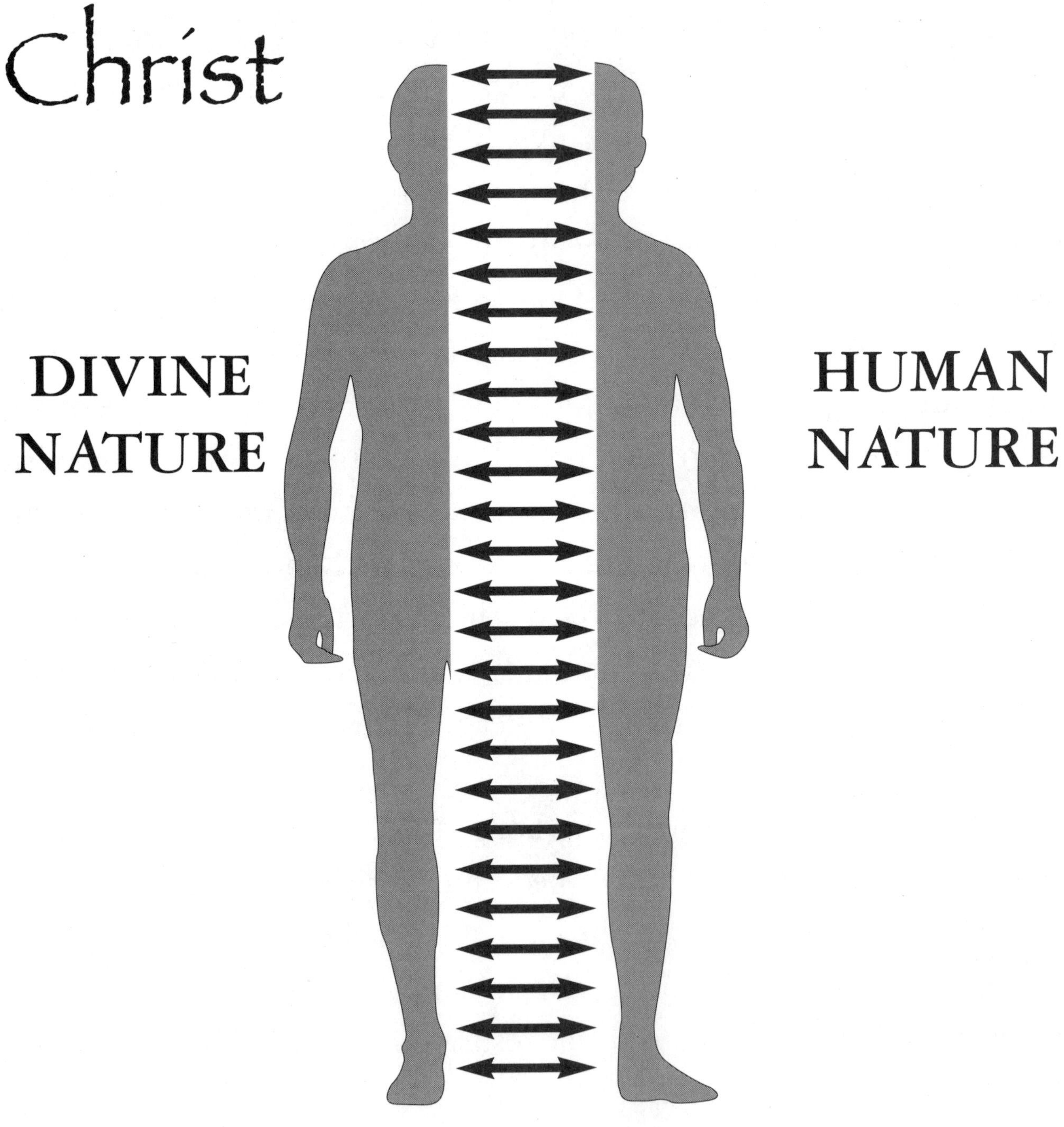

Christ

DIVINE
NATURE

HUMAN
NATURE

The controversy reached a boiling point when Nestorius, a bishop of Constantinople, affirmed Christ's full deity and humanity but denied his essential unity. He seemed to suggest that Christ had two natures with only a moral conjunction (a conjunction of will) between them, not an actual union in one person. This view was condemned at the Council of Ephesus in 431, where it was once again affirmed that Christ is one person having two natures—perfect humanity and perfect deity.

Chart 72

Eutychianism (Monophysitism) (A United Christ: Denial of Duality)

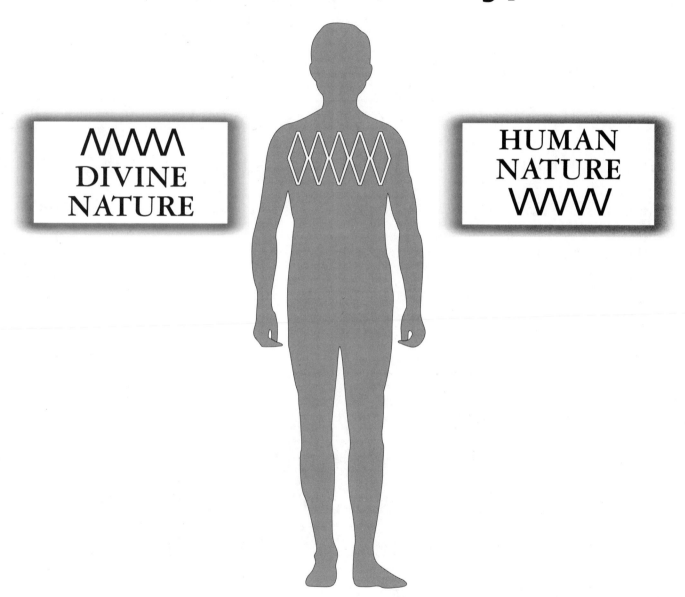

Two natures meshing to create a third, single nature

The controversy was resolved in the aftermath of the teachings of Eutyches, a churchman in Constantinople, who argued that a person must be one single nature, not two in one. While he affirmed the previous councils' declarations about Christ's unity, full humanity, and full deity, he concluded that in the incarnation Christ became one in nature. The divine and human natures coalesced into one single nature, neither divine nor human, a mixture of both in one new thing.

Chart 73

The Creed of Chalcedon (451)

[We also teach] that we apprehend this one and only Christ—Son, Lord, only-begotten—in two natures; [and we do this] without confusing the two natures, without transmuting one nature into the other, without dividing them into two separate categories, without contrasting them according to area or function. The distinctiveness of each nature is not nullified by the union. Instead, the "properties" of each nature are conserved and both natures concur in one "person" and in one essence. They are not divided or cut into two persons, but are together the one and only and only-begotten Logos of God, the Lord Jesus Christ. Thus have the prophets of old testified; thus the Lord Jesus Christ himself taught us; thus the Symbol of the Fathers has handed down to us.

Eutyches' view was condemned at the Council of Chalcedon in 451, perhaps the greatest ecumenical council in the history of the church. The subsequent creed of Chalcedon affirmed that Christ in the incarnation was fully God and fully man, in one person, without confusion forever. He is the God-man. As a true man Christ is capable of identifying with us; as God's equal he can plead our case for us.

Chart 74

The Creed of Constantinople (553)

If anyone understands by the single subsistence of our Lord Jesus Christ that it covers the meaning of many subsistences, and by this argument tries to introduce into the mystery of Christ two subsistences or two persons, and having brought in two persons; if anyone falsely represents the holy synod of Chalcedon, making out that it accepted this heretical view by its terminology of "one subsistence," and if he does not acknowledge that the Word of God is united with human flesh by subsistence, and that on account of this there is only one subsistence or one person, and that the holy synod of Chacedon thus made a formal statement of belief in the single subsistence of our Lord Jesus Christ: let him be anathema.

The meeting at Chalcedon did not end the controversy, for large segments of the church rejected the council's conclusions. Eutychians became known as Monophysites (single-nature Christologists), and their view was condemned at the fifth ecumenical council (the second council at Constantinople) in 553, out of which came the creed of Constantinople.

Chart 75

The Debate over Christology:
The Rending of the Catholic Church

The Catholic Church

The (Monophysite) Catholic Church	5 5 3	The (Chalcedonian) Catholic Church

The debate over Christology at the second Council of Constantinople eventually led to the first major schism in the Catholic Church. The church divided into two parties: dual-nature Christologists and single-nature Christologists.

Chart 76

The Divisions of the Catholic Church

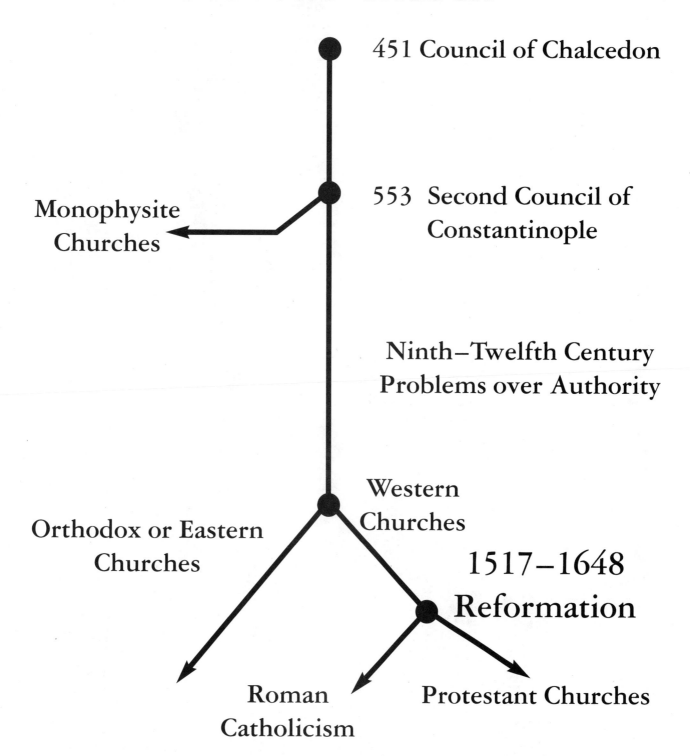

451 Council of Chalcedon

Monophysite Churches

553 Second Council of Constantinople

Ninth–Twelfth Century Problems over Authority

Western Churches

Orthodox or Eastern Churches

1517–1648 Reformation

Roman Catholicism

Protestant Churches

Three major schisms have occurred in the history of the church: the Chalcedonian–Monophysite division over the natures of Christ, the Western Catholic–Eastern Orthodox schism over authority structures, and the Roman Catholic–Protestant struggle in the Western Chalcedonian church.

Chart 77

The Life of Pelagius

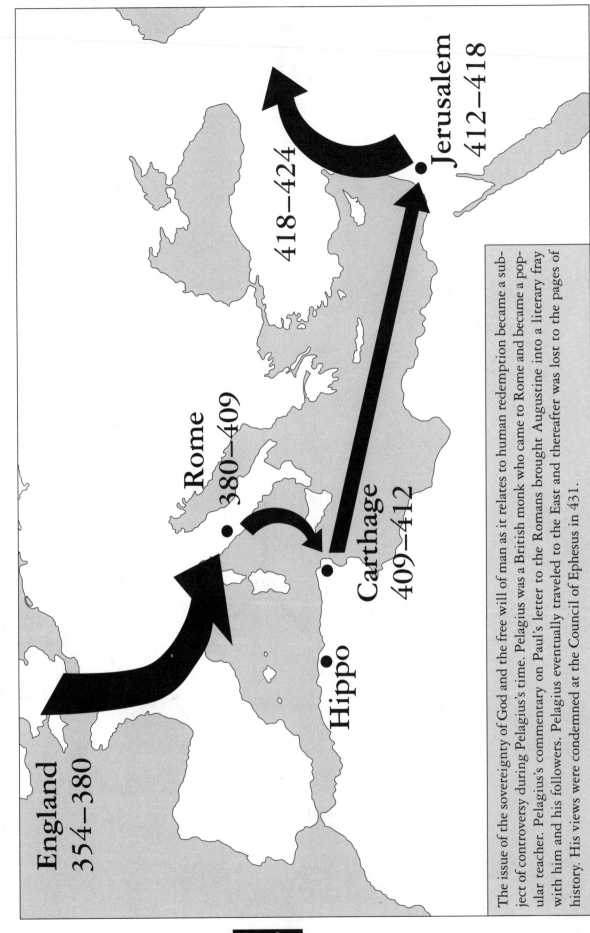

England
354–380

Rome
380–409

Hippo

Carthage
409–412

Jerusalem
412–418

418–424

The issue of the sovereignty of God and the free will of man as it relates to human redemption became a subject of controversy during Pelagius's time. Pelagius was a British monk who came to Rome and became a popular teacher. Pelagius's commentary on Paul's letter to the Romans brought Augustine into a literary fray with him and his followers. Pelagius eventually traveled to the East and thereafter was lost to the pages of history. His views were condemned at the Council of Ephesus in 431.

Chart 78

The Anthropology of Pelagius

Sin does not corrupt man's:

—Mind—
—Emotion—
—Will—

He is spiritually alive

Plenary Ability

Denial of Depravity

Pelagius taught that the fall of Adam injured neither him nor the race after him (denial of original sin). Man is born in a state of innocence and sins only insofar as it follows bad examples. The essence of sin is moral (actions), not constitutional. Man has the ability to save himself if encouraged to do so. Pelagius's message, like that of some secularists today, is a gospel of self-help.

Chart 79

The Ecclesiastical and Literary Career of Augustine

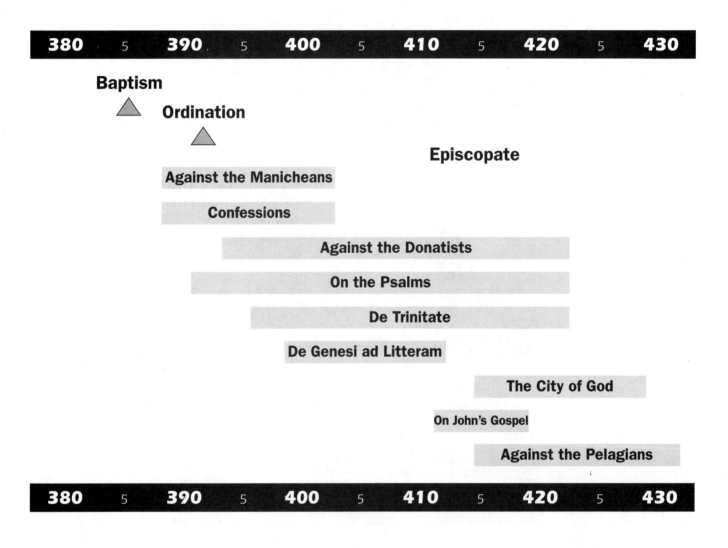

| 380 | 5 | 390 | 5 | 400 | 5 | 410 | 5 | 420 | 5 | 430 |

Baptism

Ordination

Episcopate

Against the Manicheans

Confessions

Against the Donatists

On the Psalms

De Trinitate

De Genesi ad Litteram

The City of God

On John's Gospel

Against the Pelagians

| 380 | 5 | 390 | 5 | 400 | 5 | 410 | 5 | 420 | 5 | 430 |

Augustine's ministry has shaped centuries of Christian thought. Born to a pagan father and a Christian mother and educated in rhetoric, he pursued a career at Rome, where he came under the preaching of Ambrose, bishop of Milan. After his conversion in 386 he returned to the continent of his birth (Africa), where popular acclaim brought him into the bishopric of Hippo. Three controversies occupied his literary efforts: the Manicheans, a sect he had once joined; the Donatists, a purist movement; and the Pelagians, who denied original sin.

Chart 80

The Anthropology of Augustine

Sin corrupts man's:

—Mind—
—Emotion—
—Will—

He is spiritually dead

Plenary Inability   Total Depravity

In the controversy with the Pelagians, Augustine argued that the sin of Adam had a devastating impact on him and on the entire race. Man is born into this world under the judgment of God, corrupt in nature, and completely unable and unwilling to do anything about it. Without the arbitrary grace of God, determined from eternity, the sinner is without hope of salvation.

Chart 81

Pelagius and Augustine:
A Study in Contrast

	Pelagius	**Augustine**
Original Sin	Denied	Affirmed
Natural Will	Plenary Ability	Inability
Grace	Gracious, Not Necessary	Absolute Necessity
Predestination	Based on Knowledge (foresight)	Based on Love (foreknowledge)

Pelagius and Augustine represented opposite views in terms of understanding the nature of man and the necessity of grace.

Chart 82

Pelagius and Augustine Compared

Pelagius	Augustine
Adam would have died whether he sinned or not	Sin brought death into the world
Adam's sin injured only himself	All men fell in Adam
Children are born in the state in which Adam was before his fall	Children are born guilty and depraved
The law and the gospel both lead to the kingdom of heaven	No man can enter the kingdom except through Christ
Even before the coming of the Lord there were men without sin	There is none righteous
Neither by the death and sin of Adam does the whole race die, nor by the resurrection of Christ does the whole race rise	Just as all men died in Adam, all men can be raised to life in Christ

Chart 83

Augustine on
Freedom of Choice

| Adam before the Fall | **FREEDOM** → THE GOOD / THE EVIL |

| Adam after the Fall / Unsaved mankind | **FREEDOM** → ~~THE GOOD~~ / THE EVIL |

| Saved mankind | **FREEDOM** → THE GOOD / THE EVIL |

Augustine believed that mankind always has freedom of choice, since freedom is intrinsic to being human. Unsaved and saved people alike are free to choose whatever they have available to them; however, the unsaved cannot choose Christ because he is unknown to them unless God wills through his Spirit to reveal himself to them. The problem with man is not a lack of freedom, but an object to embrace. Man is morally unable to come to Christ not because he lacks the ability to choose what he desires, but because he does not have Christ to choose.

Chart 84

Augustine's Theory of History:
The Two Cities

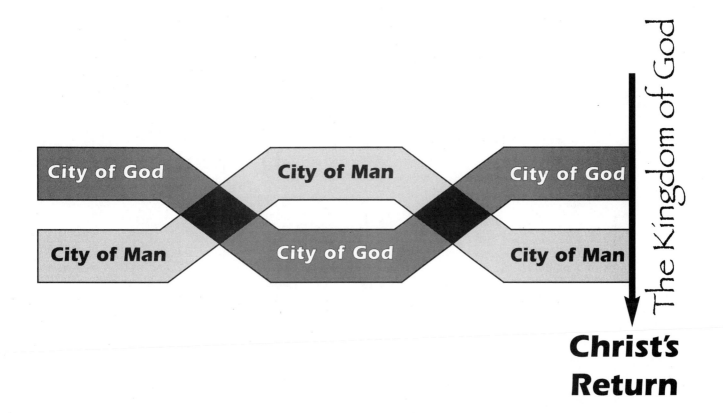

Characteristics:
- Dualism (constant struggle)
- Alienation (constant secularity)
- Denial of progress of the city of God in history
- Rejection of prophetic fulfillment in time

Augustine argued that "desire" is essential to human life; desire is neither wrong nor right in and of itself. Mankind can be divided into two groups: those who love and desire God, and those who love the world. The two are antithetical. The two kinds of love are two "cities": the "city of man" is his life and values before conversion; the "city of God" is his newfound desires. These two cities coexist in continual conflict until the end of time, when the two will be separated.

Chart 85

Augustine and the Triumph of Amillennialism

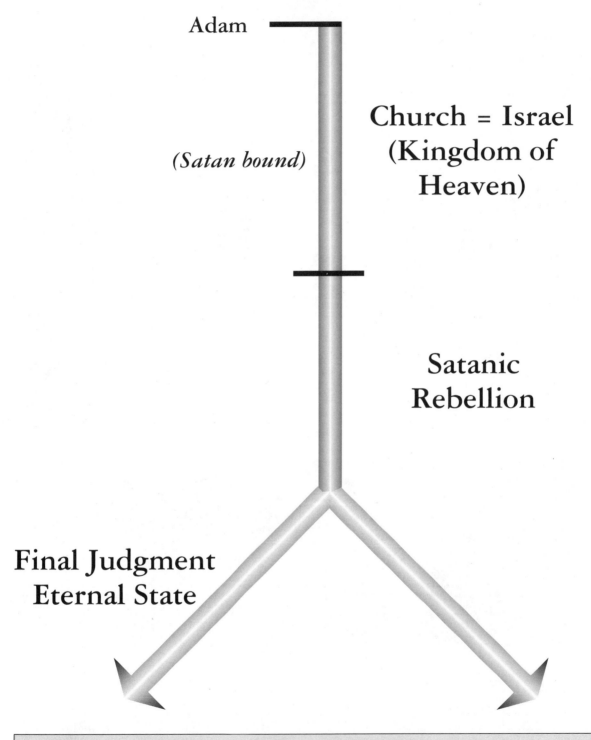

Adam

(Satan bound)

Church = Israel
(Kingdom of
Heaven)

Satanic
Rebellion

Final Judgment
Eternal State

Augustine was a proponent of an amillennial understanding of prophetic events. At the end of time Christ will return in judgment to crush his enemies and gather his chosen. Until his coming, there is no prophetic fulfillment in time, and there is no reign of Christ on earth to be anticipated. Christ does reign in the hearts of his people.

Chart 86

Augustine and the Nature of the Church

HOLINESS	MEMBERSHIP
Novatianism **249 250**	*Cyprian*
Donatism **303 311**	*Augustine*

Augustine confronted the Donatists over the nature of the church. The Donatists, like the Novatians before them, emerged during the persecution of the church in North Africa. They argued that anyone, bishop or layman, who denied the faith in order to avoid persecution should be put out of the church permanently. If the essence of the church is purity, then anyone who is not holy should not remain in the church. Augustine argued that the essence of the church was a connection to the apostolic faith, exclusively preserved in the church whose lineage can be traced to the apostles. Thus, there is no salvation outside the church because the church possesses the sacred deposit of the gospel.

Chart 87

The Development of Monasticism

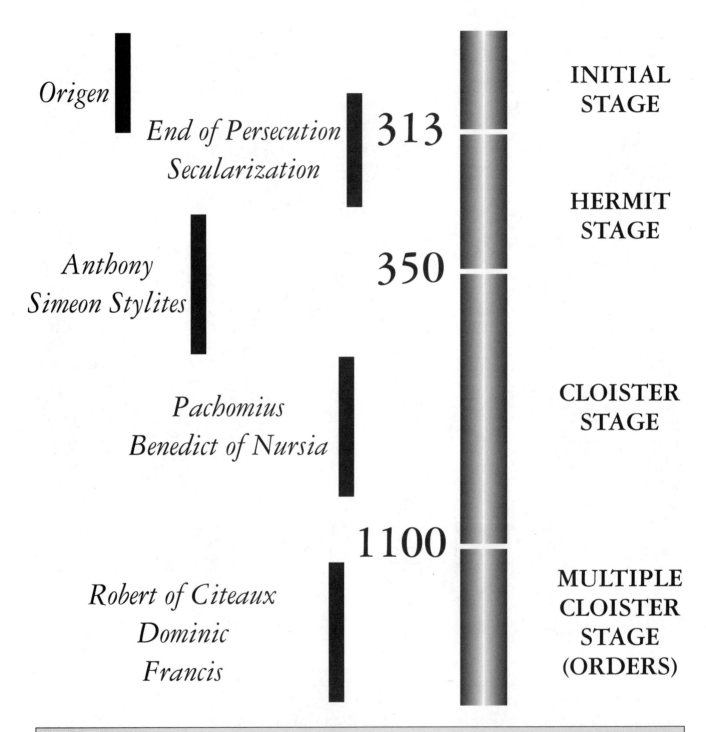

Origen

End of Persecution
Secularization

313

Anthony
Simeon Stylites

350

Pachomius
Benedict of Nursia

1100

Robert of Citeaux
Dominic
Francis

INITIAL STAGE

HERMIT STAGE

CLOISTER STAGE

MULTIPLE CLOISTER STAGE (ORDERS)

The church's quest for single-minded devotion to God led to various forms of societal rejection. Monasticism is the most celebrated form of separatist spirituality. The monastic ideal developed gradually, particularly after persecution ended in the fourth century. Various individuals sought the secluded life of study and meditation, combined with subsistence living. Later, monks formed communities following the Benedictine vow. Eventually, large monastic orders emerged, such as the Cistercians, Franciscans, and Dominicans.

Chart 88

John Cassian and Cooperative Grace

Sin hinders man's:

—Mind—
—Emotion—
—Will—

He needs help

Causative Cooperative Ability

Denial of Total Corruption (Deprivation, Not Depravity)

John Cassian, a proponent of monasticism, sought to reform what he saw as the excesses of both the Augustinian and Pelagian approaches to sin and grace. Cassian suggested that Adam's sin did not have the devastating effect proposed by Augustine, though it was more serious than the Pelagians taught. Sin had a debilitating but not devastating effect. Man in the lost state can cooperate with God. God does certain things, but man must do other things—things as much the cause of salvation as what God does.

Chart 89

Divine Grace and the Synod of Orange (529)

Sin corrupts man's:

—Mind—
—Emotion—
—Will—

He is spiritually dead

Plenary Inability   **Total Depravity**

Stress on Human Action

In 529 the Synod of Orange addressed Cassian's view. While the synod condemned Cassianism and Pelagianism, it failed to completely endorse the Augustinian idea of predestination. The synod's ambivalence on the issue of divine determinism caused confusion that would reverberate through the centuries.

Chart 90

Basic Views in the Sin-and-Grace Controversy

Augustine	Salvation Totally and Causally of God
Synod of Orange (Semi-Augustinianism)	Salvation Originates in God and Proceeds by God and Man
Cassian (Semi-Pelagianism)	Salvation Originates in Man and Proceeds by Man and God
Pelagius	Salvation Totally and Causally of Man

The differences between the major views of sin's effect on mankind and the place of human ability in salvation have important implications for understanding the confusion in the late medieval church and the rise of the reform movements in the sixteenth century.

Chart 91

Basic Views of
Grace Summarized

Pelagianism | Pelagius, Julian of Eclanum, Coelestius |

Man is born essentially good and capable of doing what is necessary for salvation.

Augustinianism | Augustine of Hippo |

Man is dead in sin; salvation is totally by the grace of God, which is given only to the elect.

Semi-Pelagianism | John Cassian |

The grace of God and the will of man work together in salvation, in which man must take the initiative.

Semi-Augustinianism | Caesarius of Arles |

The grace of God comes to all, enabling a person to choose and perform what is necessary for salvation.

Chart 92

Early Medieval Christianity and Baptism

> " He saved us through
> the washing of rebirth
> and renewal by
> the Holy Spirit."
>
> Titus 3:5

Physical birth
Spiritual birth

Spiritual rebirth

Eucharist

Water and spiritual
baptism

Confirmation

Regeneration

Conversion

Symbol  Reality

With the empire's official embrace of Christianity, the church's understanding of baptism was reconfigured. At birth people became members of the state, and at baptism they became members of the church. However, being a church member did not mean that one was saved. Baptism became an anticipatory symbol of true faith expressed at confirmation when one entered the spiritual church.

Chart 93

The Medieval Period
of Church History
(from 600 to 1500)

The Emerging Power of the Medieval Church

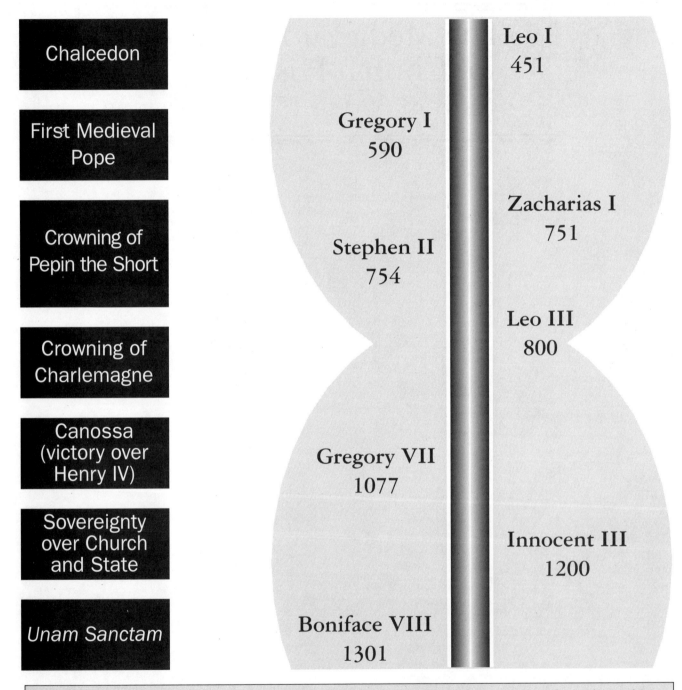

Chalcedon

First Medieval Pope

Crowning of Pepin the Short

Crowning of Charlemagne

Canossa (victory over Henry IV)

Sovereignty over Church and State

Unam Sanctam

Leo I
451

Gregory I
590

Zacharias I
751

Stephen II
754

Leo III
800

Gregory VII
1077

Innocent III
1200

Boniface VIII
1301

A major theme throughout the medieval period is the increasing power of the church and its relationship to the power of the state. Perhaps due to the authority vacuum created by the demise of the Roman Empire, medieval popes wielded greater and greater authority. Popes crowned monarchs in the Carolingian Era (eighth–early eleventh centuries), Gregory VII triumphed momentarily over Henry IV of Germany, Innocent III humbled the kings of England and France, and Boniface VIII made the most strident claims of the church's supremacy over the state.

Chart 94

The Rise of Episcopacy and Papacy in the Church

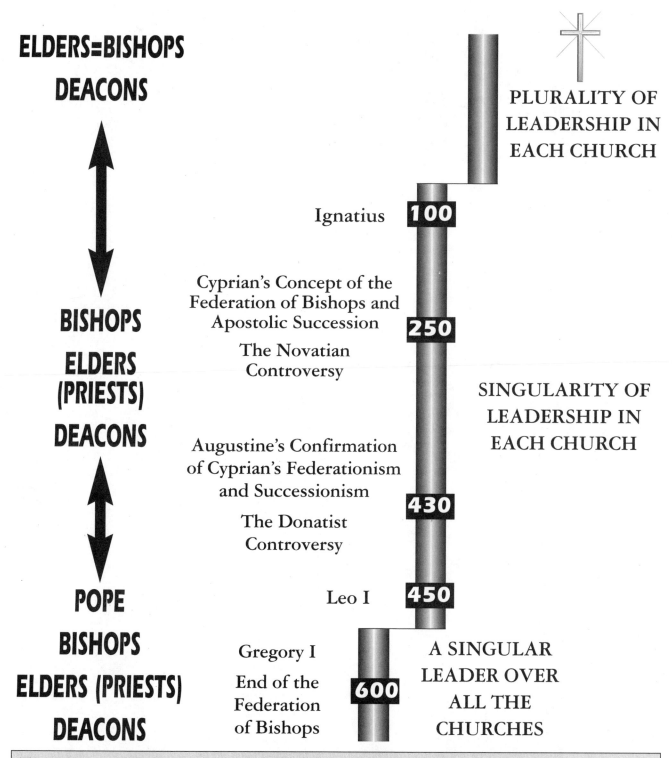

ELDERS=BISHOPS

DEACONS

PLURALITY OF LEADERSHIP IN EACH CHURCH

Ignatius **100**

BISHOPS

ELDERS (PRIESTS)

DEACONS

Cyprian's Concept of the Federation of Bishops and Apostolic Succession **250**

The Novatian Controversy

SINGULARITY OF LEADERSHIP IN EACH CHURCH

Augustine's Confirmation of Cyprian's Federationism and Successionism **430**

The Donatist Controversy

Leo I **450**

POPE

BISHOPS

ELDERS (PRIESTS)

DEACONS

Gregory I **600**

End of the Federation of Bishops

A SINGULAR LEADER OVER ALL THE CHURCHES

The medieval period saw the emergence of a singular head over the churches in the West, a view that was never acknowledged in the East. The idea that the bishops functioned in a community of equals, a confederation with a quasi-episcopal rule, gave way in Gregory the Great to the papacy.

Chart 95

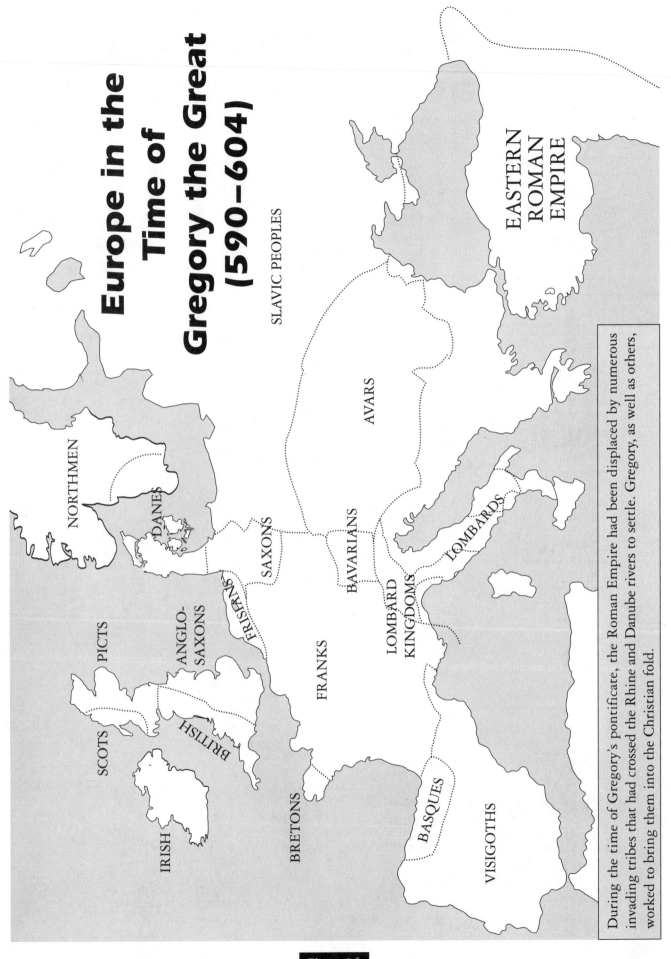

Europe in the Time of Gregory the Great (590–604)

SLAVIC PEOPLES

NORTHMEN

DANES

SAXONS

AVARS

EASTERN ROMAN EMPIRE

LOMBARDS

BAVARIANS

FRISIANS

LOMBARD KINGDOMS

SCOTS

PICTS

ANGLO-SAXONS

BRITISH

IRISH

FRANKS

BRETONS

BASQUES

VISIGOTHS

During the time of Gregory's pontificate, the Roman Empire had been displaced by numerous invading tribes that had crossed the Rhine and Danube rivers to settle. Gregory, as well as others, worked to bring them into the Christian fold.

Chart 96

The Medieval Church:
Social Disintegration and Religious Renewal

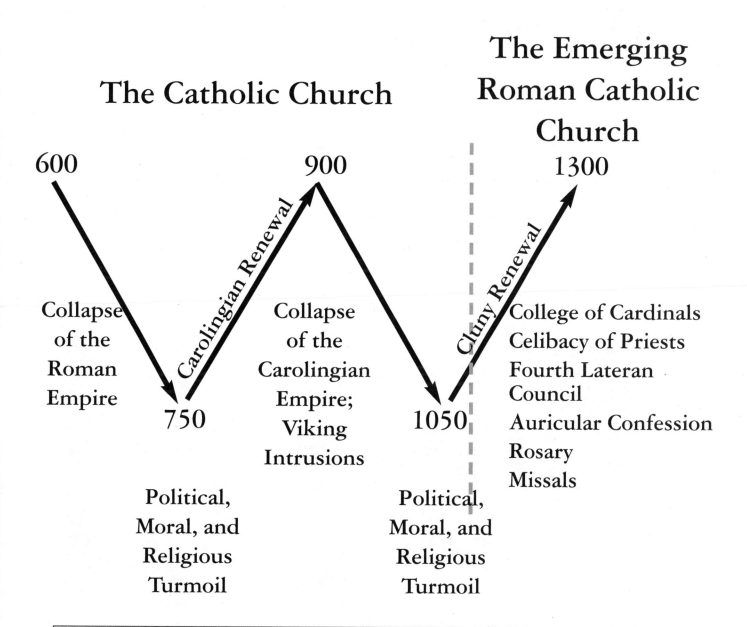

The Catholic Church

The Emerging Roman Catholic Church

600

900

1300

Carolingian Renewal

Cluny Renewal

Collapse of the Roman Empire

Collapse of the Carolingian Empire; Viking Intrusions

College of Cardinals

Celibacy of Priests

Fourth Lateran Council

Auricular Confession

Rosary

Missals

750

1050

Political, Moral, and Religious Turmoil

Political, Moral, and Religious Turmoil

The Catholic Church began to change, with the more significant alterations coming in the context of the church's recovery from the decline of the Carolingian Empire and the unsettling effect of Viking intrusions. Political chaos was accompanied by religious decadence. The eleventh-century Cluny reform movement brought the return of the church's fortunes in a positive sense, but it was also a time that witnessed a decline of the notions of divine grace and human inability. While the Roman Catholic Church did not begin at that time, the seeds of the movement were being planted.

Chart 97

The History of the Doctrine of Salvation in the Ancient and Medieval Church

The Old Catholic Church

The New Catholic Church

AUGUSTINE	SYNOD OF ORANGE	PETER LOMBARD THOMAS AQUINAS	BONIFACE VIII
430	529	1223	1305
Sola gratia	Confirmed Augustinianism. Condemned Cassianism and Pelagianism	Semi-Augustinianism Cassianism	*Unam sanctam* Submission to Pope Necessary for Salvation

Two Sacraments= Symbols of Inward Grace

Eucharist and Baptism

Seven Sacraments= Symbols That Contain and Confer Grace (Merit)

(*Ex opere operato*)

Baptism, Confirmation, Eucharist, Penance, Unction, Orders, Matrimony

The most important change that began to turn the Catholic Church toward an increasingly Roman Catholic posture was the drift of the church away from the Augustinian doctrines of human inability and the necessity of divine grace. The sacraments, regardless of whether divine grace or human effort had priority, came to be regarded as the means of grace for the believer. Viewing the sacraments as having an objective rather than a subjective function indicated the tendency of churchmen to affirm the later avowed Roman Catholic understanding of salvation.

Chart 98

The Emergence of the Roman Catholic Church

Latin used in prayer and worship, imposed by Pope Gregory I	600
Prayers directed to Mary, dead saints, and angels	600
Kissing pope's feet began with Pope Constantine	709
Veneration of cross, images, and relics authorized	786
College of Cardinals established	927
Canonization of dead people as saints initiated	995
Attendance at Mass made mandatory	1000
Celibacy of priesthood, decreed by Pope Gregory VII	1079
Rosary, repetitious praying with beads, invented by Peter the Hermit	1090
The sale of indulgences established to reduce time in purgatory	1190
Transubstantiation, proclaimed by Pope Innocent III	1215
Confession of sins to priests, instituted by Pope Innocent III	1215
The doctrine of seven sacraments affirmed	1439
Tradition claimed equal in authority with the Bible, Council of Trent	1545
Apocryphal books declared canon by Council of Trent	1546

Slowly, ever so slowly, the pieces came together to create the mosaic of Roman Catholicism.

Chart 99

The Development of Roman Catholic Theology

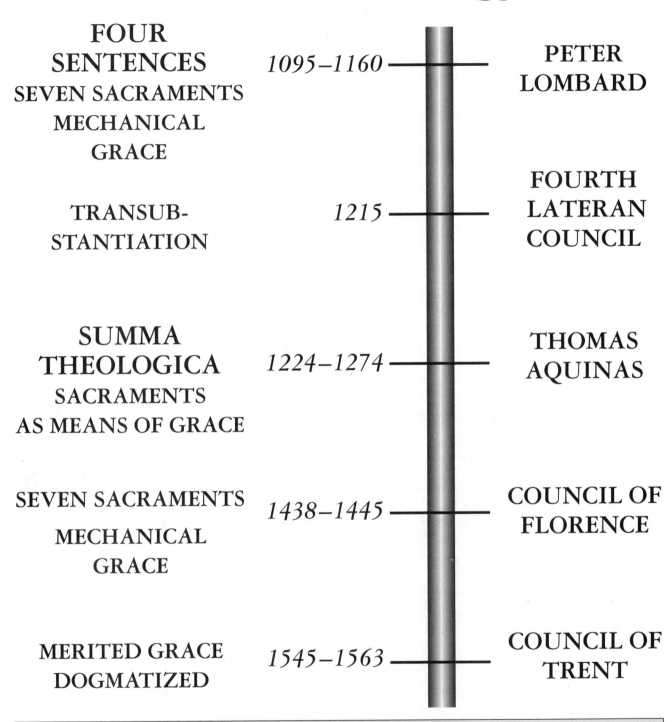

FOUR SENTENCES
SEVEN SACRAMENTS
MECHANICAL GRACE

1095–1160 — PETER LOMBARD

TRANSUB-STANTIATION

1215 — FOURTH LATERAN COUNCIL

SUMMA THEOLOGICA
SACRAMENTS AS MEANS OF GRACE

1224–1274 — THOMAS AQUINAS

SEVEN SACRAMENTS
MECHANICAL GRACE

1438–1445 — COUNCIL OF FLORENCE

MERITED GRACE DOGMATIZED

1545–1563 — COUNCIL OF TRENT

Peter Lombard and Thomas Aquinas argued that sacraments were necessary for salvation because God's grace was dispensed through them. The Fourth Lateran Council declared the Eucharist to be the true body and blood of Christ. The Council of Florence was the first authoritative gathering that declared not only that the sacraments were seven in number, but also that grace is dispensed through the sacraments apart from the attitude of the participant.

Chart 100

Political Structures in the Medieval Period

MEROVINGIAN DYNASTY (476–750)
CAROLINGIAN DYNASTY (750–843)

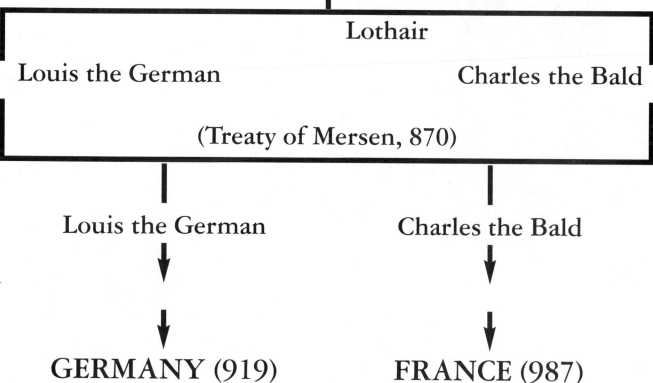

Charles Martel

Pepin the Short

Charlemagne

Louis the Pious

(Treaty of Verdun, 843)

Lothair

Louis the German | Charles the Bald

(Treaty of Mersen, 870)

Louis the German | Charles the Bald

GERMANY (919) | **FRANCE (987)**

Of the tribes that displaced the Roman Empire in Europe, the Franks dominated, establishing a kingdom that crossed several centuries. Initially the Merovingians ruled, but in time the weak kings were replaced with the Carolingians. Under these kings, particularly Charlemagne (Charles the Great), the kingdom was expanded. After Charlemagne's death, the empire was divided among competing sons. As uncertain times resulted from the decline of these kings, the foundation of the modern nation-states of Germany and France were established.

Chart 101

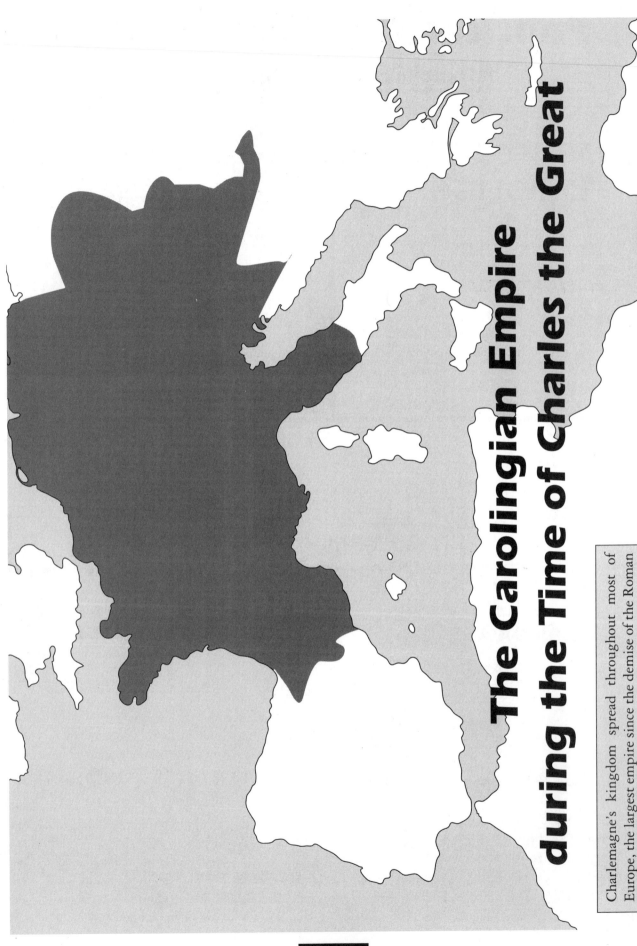

The Carolingian Empire during the Time of Charles the Great

Charlemagne's kingdom spread throughout most of Europe, the largest empire since the demise of the Roman Empire in the fifth century.

Chart 102

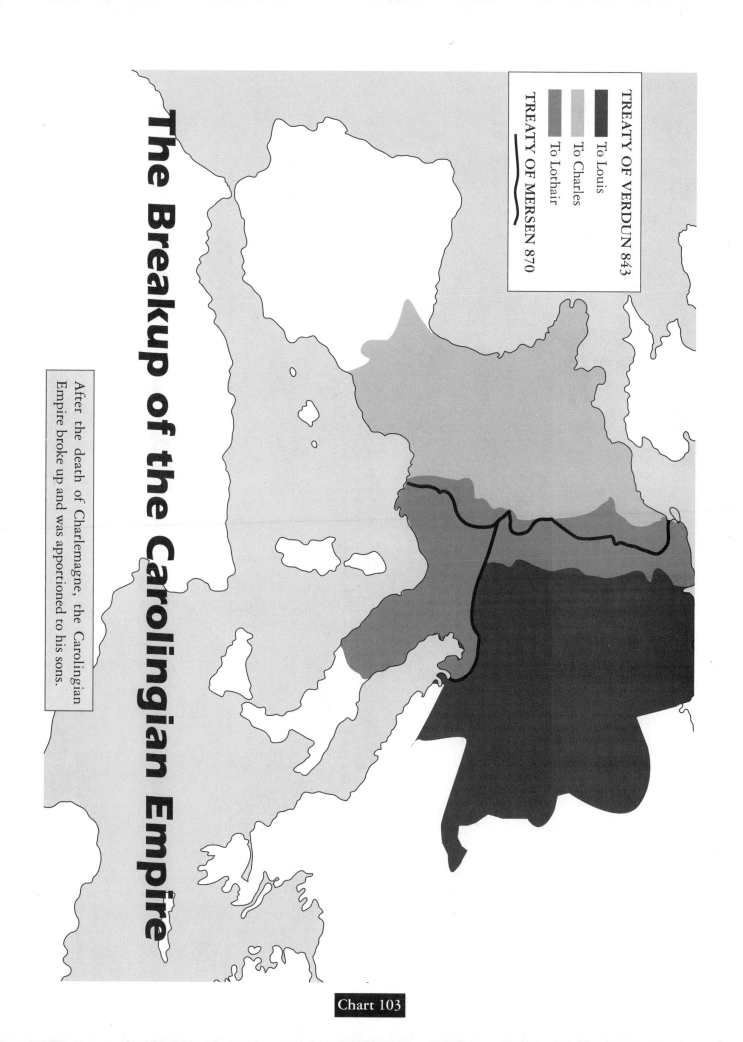

The Breakup of the Carolingian Empire

After the death of Charlemagne, the Carolingian Empire broke up and was apportioned to his sons.

TREATY OF VERDUN 843

- To Louis
- To Charles
- To Lothair

TREATY OF MERSEN 870

Chart 103

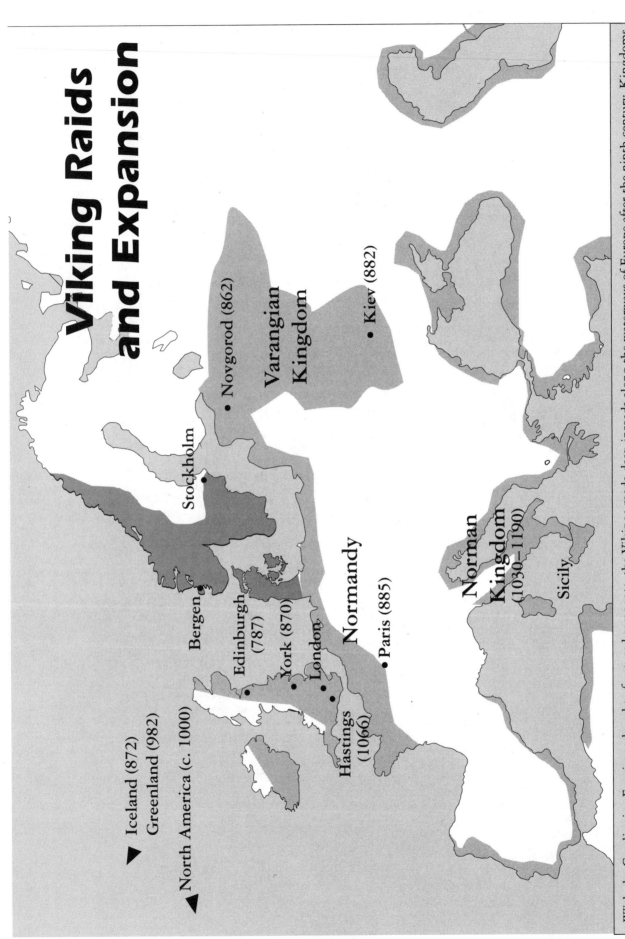

Viking Raids and Expansion

Iceland (872)
Greenland (982)

North America (c. 1000)

Bergen

Stockholm

Edinburgh (787)

York (870)

London

Hastings (1066)

Normandy

Paris (885)

Novgorod (862)

Varangian
Kingdom

Kiev (882)

Norman
Kingdom
(1030–1190)

Sicily

With the Carolingian Empire reduced to fractured remnants, the Vikings made deep inroads along the waterways of Europe after the ninth century. Kingdoms were established in Normandy and on Sicily in the Mediterranean. In this era they penetrated to the Caspian and Black seas, as well as to North America.

Chart 104

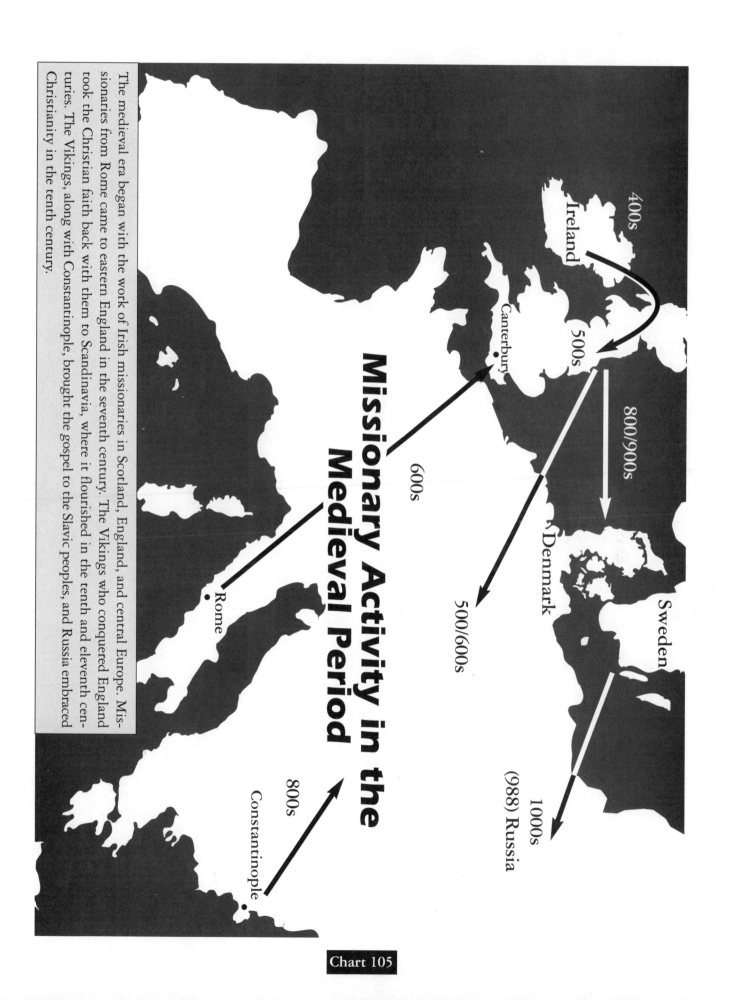

Missionary Activity in the Medieval Period

400s

Ireland

500s

Canterbury

600s

800/900s

Denmark

500/600s

Sweden

1000s
(988) Russia

Rome

800

Constantinople

The medieval era began with the work of Irish missionaries in Scotland, England, and central Europe. Missionaries from Rome came to eastern England in the seventh century. The Vikings who conquered England took the Christian faith back with them to Scandinavia, where it flourished in the tenth and eleventh centuries. The Vikings, along with Constantinople, brought the gospel to the Slavic peoples, and Russia embraced Christianity in the tenth century.

Chart 105

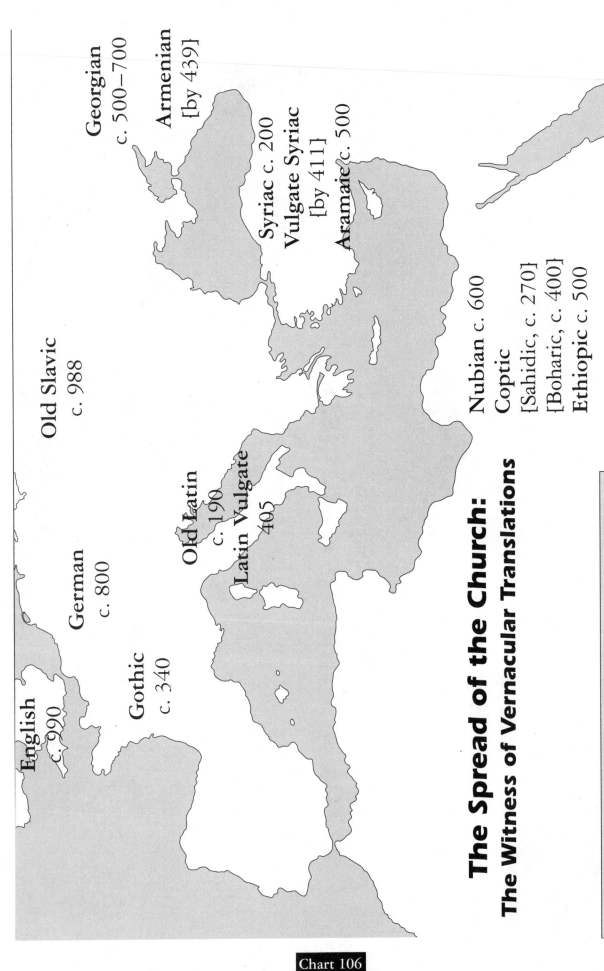

English
c. 990

Old Slavic
c. 988

Georgian
c. 500–700

Armenian
[by 439]

German
c. 800

Gothic
c. 340

Old Latin
c. 190

Latin Vulgate
405

Syriac c. 200
Vulgate Syriac
[by 411]
Aramaic c. 500

Nubian c. 600
Coptic
[Sahidic, c. 270]
[Boharic, c. 400]
Ethiopic c. 500

The Spread of the Church:
The Witness of Vernacular Translations

The progress of the gospel can be traced by the development of translations
of the Scriptures into the languages of many different peoples.

Chart 106

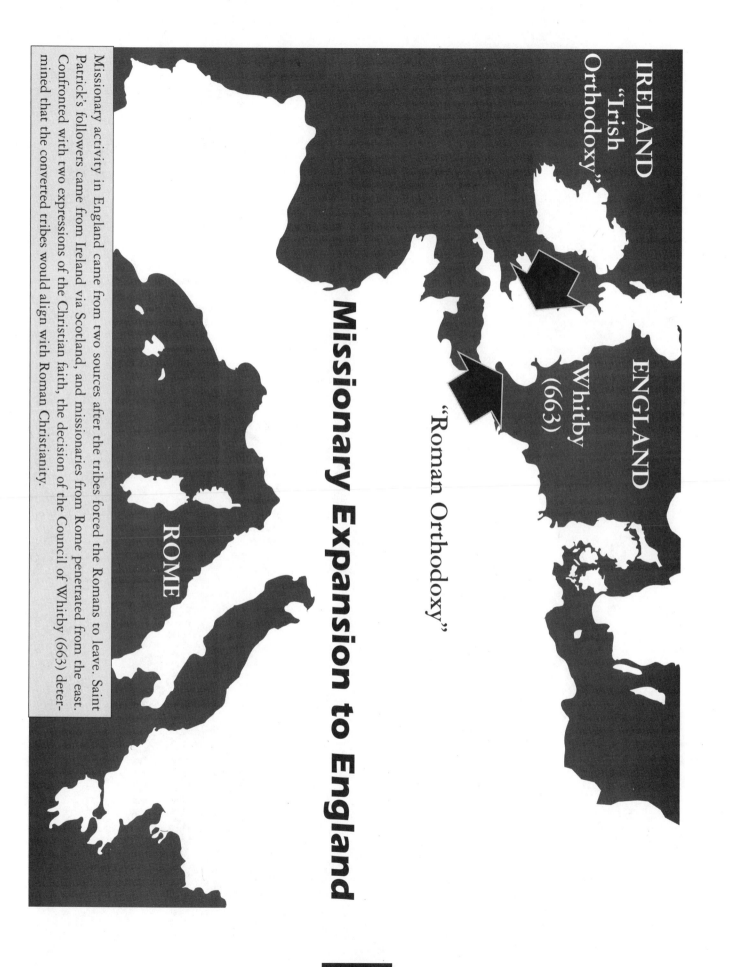

Missionary Expansion to England

IRELAND
"Irish Orthodoxy"

ENGLAND

Whitby (663)

"Roman Orthodoxy"

ROME

Missionary activity in England came from two sources after the tribes forced the Romans to leave. Saint Patrick's followers came from Ireland via Scotland, and missionaries from Rome penetrated from the east. Confronted with two expressions of the Christian faith, the decision of the Council of Whitby (663) determined that the converted tribes would align with Roman Christianity.

Chart 107

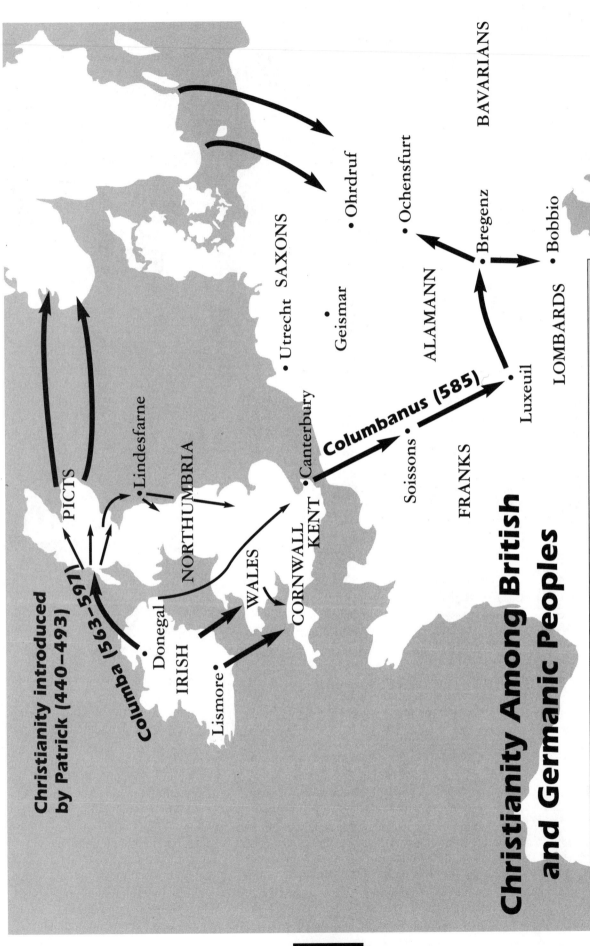

Christianity Among British and Germanic Peoples

BAVARIANS

• Ohrdruf

• Ochensfurt

Bregenz •

• Bobbio

SAXONS

Utrecht •

• Geismar

ALAMANN

LOMBARDS

Luxeuil •

Columbanus (585)

Canterbury •

Soissons •

FRANKS

KENT

• Lindesfarne

NORTHUMBRIA

PICTS

Columba (563–597)

WALES

CORNWALL

Donegal •

IRISH

Lismore •

Christianity introduced by Patrick (440–493)

Patrick's efforts to convert the Irish to Christianity was successful. His work spawned an aggressive missionary enterprise that resulted in the founding of the monastery of Iona, which fostered greater missionary activity. Columba brought the gospel to Scotland, Aidan into England, and Columbanus to central Europe.

Chart 108

The Rise of the
Islamic Faith

The History of Islam

570	Birth of Muhammad
622	the Hijrah
630	the capture of Mecca
632	the death of Muhammad
636	the conquest of Jerusalem and Damascus
690	the construction of the Dome of the Rock, Jerusalem
713	the conquest of Cordova, Spain, and the expansion into the Indus Valley
732	the Battle of Tours, France
1099	the capture of Jerusalem by the Crusaders
1453	the fall of Constantinople

The latest of the world religions, Islam is a faith based on the revelations of Muhammad recorded in the Koran. The Hijrah (the flight of the prophet from Mecca to Medina) is the date from which the Islamic calendar begins.

Chart 109

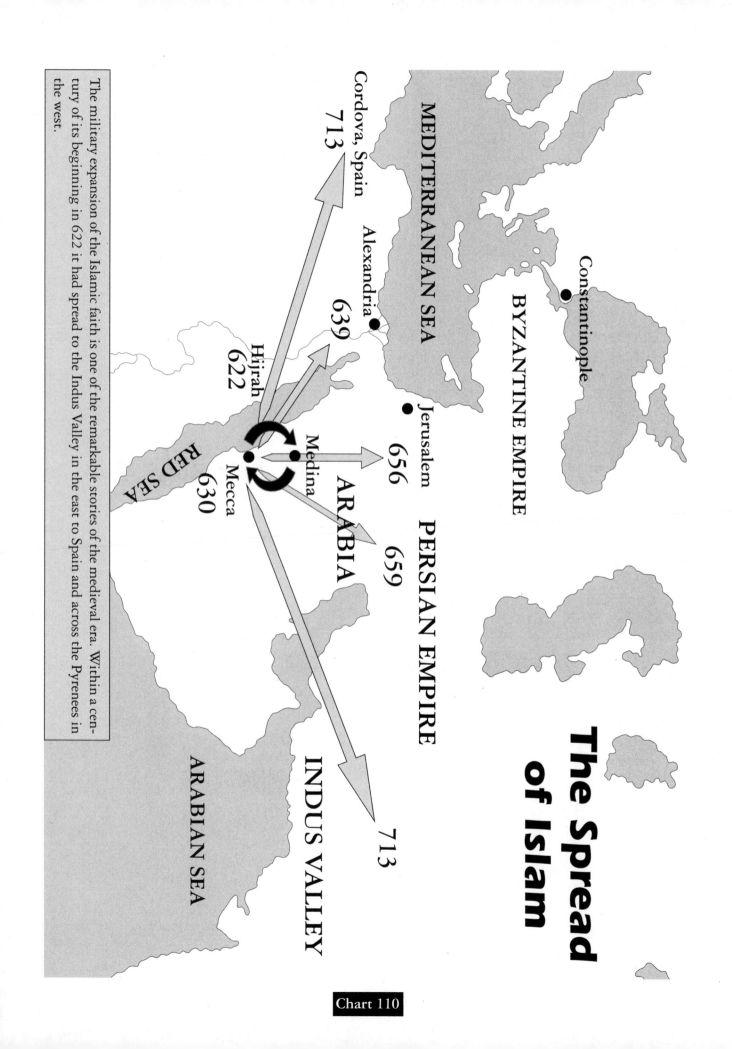

The Spread of Islam

MEDITERRANEAN SEA

BYZANTINE EMPIRE

Constantinople

Cordova, Spain
713

Alexandria
639

Jerusalem
656

Hijrah
622

Medina

Mecca

630

RED SEA

ARABIA

PERSIAN EMPIRE

659

INDUS VALLEY

713

ARABIAN SEA

The military expansion of the Islamic faith is one of the remarkable stories of the medieval era. Within a century of its beginning in 622 it had spread to the Indus Valley in the east to Spain and across the Pyrenees in the west.

Chart 110

The Five Pillars of Islam

Profession of Allah

Prayer   *5 times daily*

Alms   *2.5%*

Fasting   *Ramadan*

Pilgrimage   *Mecca*

"The role of Islam in relation to all other faiths is to prune, correct, purge, and complete them."
(The House of Islam, 7)

The essence of Islamic religion is obedience or submission (the meaning of the term *islam*). The faith is expressed in a strident monotheism, structured prayer, mandated giving to the poor, fasting during the daylight hours of Ramadan, and a pilgrimage to Mecca (the holiest of Muslim sites).

Chart 111

The Continuing
Christological Controversy

Monothelitism
(A Denial of Christ's Humanity)

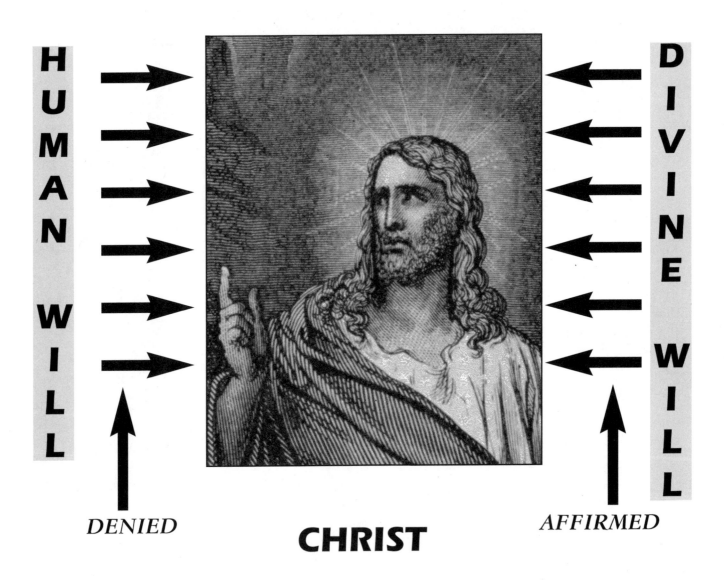

HUMAN WILL

DIVINE WILL

DENIED

CHRIST

AFFIRMED

The Christological controversies waged in the fourth and fifth centuries continued in the seventh century. The aggressive Islamic threat brought the need to resolve the Monophysite controversy and unify the divided church. The essence of the issue was whether or not Christ had two wills—divine and human—or one will—a divine one. The issue seemed to be the same one that troubled the church in the Apollinarian controversy: If Christ had only a divine will, how could he be said to be truly human?

Chart 112

The Creed of Constantinople (680)

And we likewise preach *two natural wills* in him [Jesus Christ], and *two natural operations* undivided, inconvertible, inseparable, unmixed, according to the doctrine of the holy fathers; and the two natural wills [are] not contrary (as the impious heretics assert), far from it! But his human will follows the divine will, and is not resisting or reluctant, but rather subject to his divine and omnipotent will. For it was proper that the will of the flesh should be moved, but be subjected to the divine will, according to the wise Athanasius. For as his flesh is called and is the flesh of the God Logos, so is also the natural will of his flesh the proper will of the Logos, as he says himself: "I came from heaven not to do my own will but the will of the Father who sent me" (John 6:38). . . . Therefore we confess two natural wills and operations, harmoniously united for the salvation of the human race.

The sixth ecumenical council (the third at Constantinople) condemned the Monothelites, the single-will Christologists, arguing instead that Christ possessed two perfect wills—one divine and one human.

Chart 113

The Division of the Church:
West and East

Constantine's New Capital:
The Seeds of Division

Constantinople

Rome

The seeds for the later division of the church into Western Catholicism and Eastern Catholicism were sown by Constantine in 325 when he formed a second capital (Constantinople) in the East.

Chart 114

The *Filioque* Controversy

Eastern Church	Latin Church

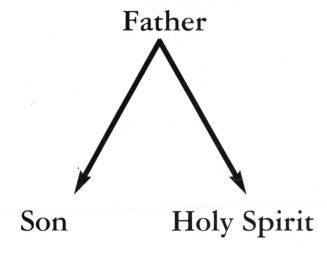

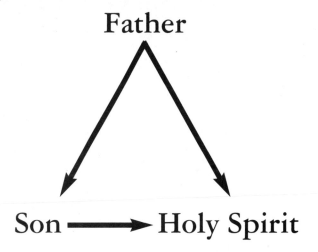

The Holy Spirit proceeds
from the Father

The Holy Spirit proceeds
from the Father and
the Son *(filioque)*

Another issue that brought tension in the church was the *filioque* clause ("and the Son") inserted in the Nicene Creed in 589 in the West. One key question was the authority of an ecumenical council's decrees; the Eastern Fathers viewed them as sacred. Thus, beneath the debate of whether the Son sent the Spirit into the world was the issue of the authority of the creeds and the role of the Western pontiff in Eastern affairs. Eventually both parties accused the other of heresy.

Chart 115

The History of the Orthodox Church:
An Eastern Perspective

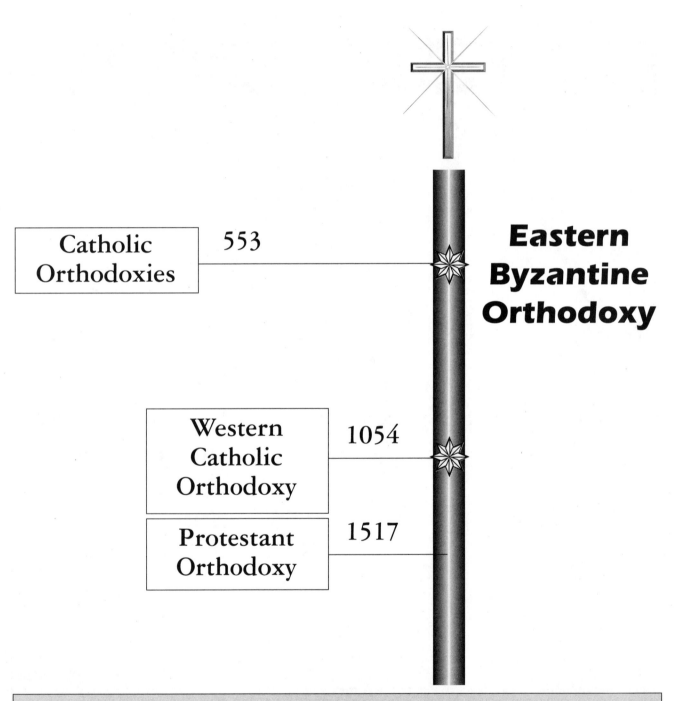

Catholic
Orthodoxies

553

**Eastern
Byzantine
Orthodoxy**

Western
Catholic
Orthodoxy

1054

Protestant
Orthodoxy

1517

From the perspective of the Eastern church fathers, the Western churchmen misunderstood history. Since the church began in the East, the Orthodox Church is the original church. Monophysites and the later Western Catholic Church are viewed as factions from the original.

Chart 116

The Debate over Authority:
The Rending of the (Chalcedonian) Catholic Church

The Catholic Church

The (Monophysite) Catholic Church	The Eastern (Byzantine) Orthodox Church

The (Chalcedonian) Catholic Church	The Western Catholic Church

The division of the Catholic Church into Eastern Orthodoxy and Western Catholicism in 1054 is the second major division in the professing Christian Church. The underlying issue seems to have been the increasing authority of the church in the West over Eastern ecclesiastical affairs.

Chart 117

The Crusades

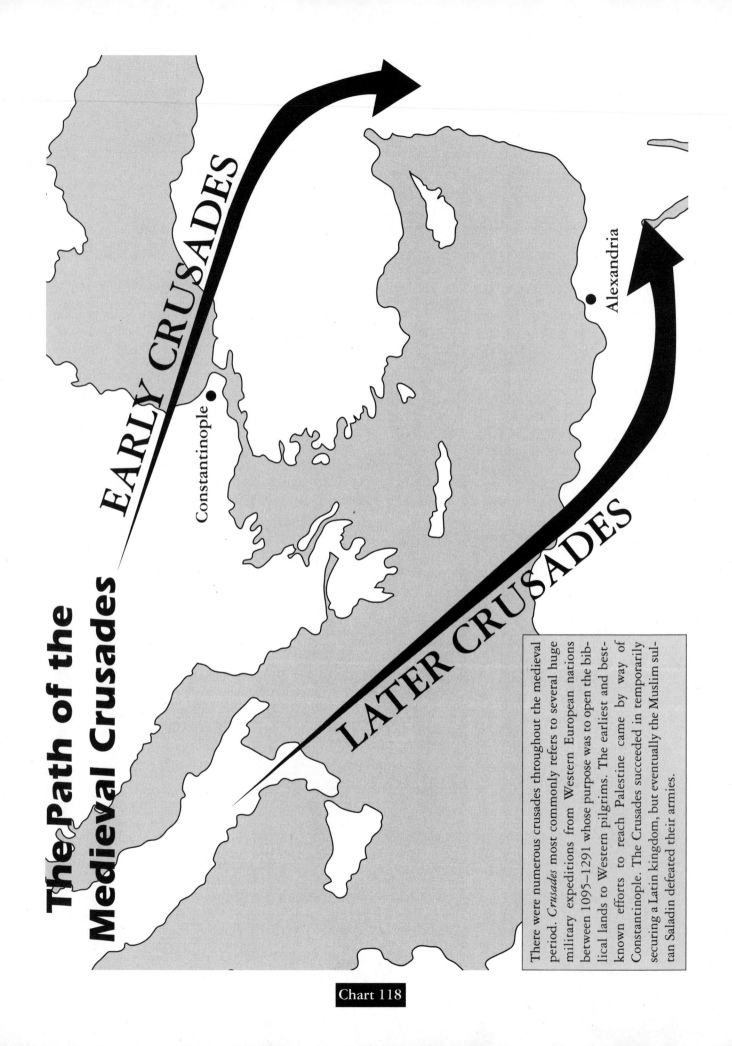

The Path of the Medieval Crusades

EARLY CRUSADES

LATER CRUSADES

Constantinople

Alexandria

There were numerous crusades throughout the medieval period. *Crusades* most commonly refers to several huge military expeditions from Western European nations between 1095–1291 whose purpose was to open the biblical lands to Western pilgrims. The earliest and best-known efforts to reach Palestine came by way of Constantinople. The Crusades succeeded in temporarily securing a Latin kingdom, but eventually the Muslim sultan Saladin defeated their armies.

Chart 118

The Crusades and the Kingdom of Jerusalem

- Tyre
- Akko (Acre)
- Tiberias
- Caesarea
- Jaffa
- Jerusalem

The Latin kingdom was destroyed by Muslim armies, and the Crusader Period ended in 1291 when the last of the Crusaders left Akko, the maritime capital of the Crusader kingdom.

Chart 119

Monasticism

The Major Monasteries
of the Middle Ages

The monastic ideal for the cultivation of spirituality was a potent force in Catholicism from the fourth century on. In the early medieval period the monasteries at Iona and Lindisfarne became famous as missionary training and learning centers. Perhaps the most famous medieval monastery, Monte Cassino, was founded by Benedict of Nursia in 529. In the middle medieval period the reforming monastery at Cluny was established and became a model for several cloisters that emerged in the same period.

Chart 120

The Religious Orders of the Medieval Period

NAME	FOUNDER	EMPHASIS
Benedictines	Benedict of Nursia (480–547)	Founded at Monte Cassino (c. 529). Cultivated intellectual and spiritual life according to the Rule of Saint Benedict (vow of poverty, regular liturgical practice, physical labor, theological/spiritual training).
Cistercians	Robert of Citeaux	Founded at Citeaux (1098). Followed Rule of Saint Benedict more strictly.
Cluny	William, Duke of Aquitaine	Broke away from the Benedictines. Sought out care for the poor.
Dominicans	Dominic of Osma (1170–1221)	One of the mendicant ("begging") orders. Took vows of poverty, and stressed the importance of preaching, missions, and theological training.
Franciscans	Francis of Assisi (c. 1181–1226)	One of the mendicant ("begging") orders. Renunciation of worldly goods and commitment to theological training.

Among the monastic orders to emerge in the medieval period were the Cistercians, founded by Robert of Citeaux (an order made famous by Bernard of Clairvaux); the Franciscans, founded by Saint Francis; and the Dominicans, founded by Saint Dominic.

Chart 121

Scholasticism

The Rise of Scholasticism

Schools in Monastic Communities

Multiplication of Cathedral Schools

Rise of Universities

Dialectic method
- Anselm
- Abelard
- Lombard

New class of professional teachers

Emergence of Aristotelian corpus and philosophy
- Aquinas

The developing European economic stabilization, as well as confrontation with the Islamic faith, led to the emergence of a new model of education in the medieval period. The rise of the university, coupled with the decline of monastic education, brought a change in the education of monks and priests from a pietistic model of prayer, Bible readings, and cultivating the spiritual disciplines to an emphasis on developing the mind through argumentation.

Chart 122

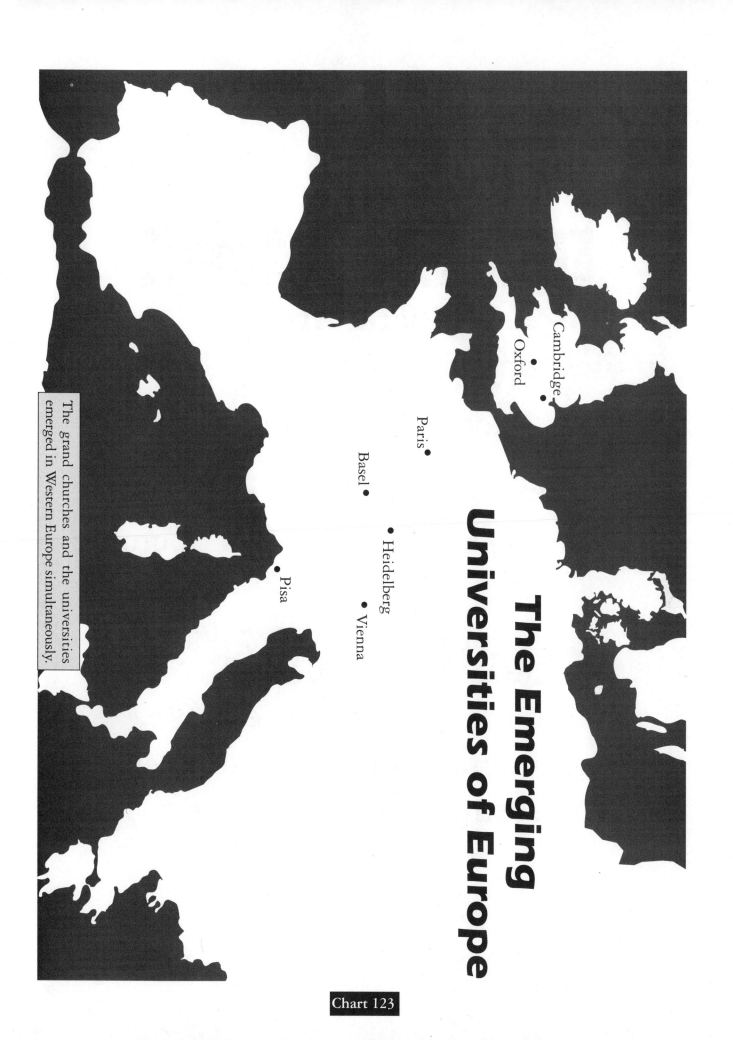

The Emerging Universities of Europe

Cambridge

Oxford

Paris

Basel

Heidelberg

Vienna

Pisa

The grand churches and the universities emerged in Western Europe simultaneously.

Chart 123

University Curricula

Educational Process

Liberal Arts
(philosophy, humanities, and the like)

Bachelor of the Bible

Bachelor of the Sentences

Master (synonymous with doctor)

Academic Exercises

Commentaries on the Bible,
commentary on the Sentences,
sermons, disputations

The emphasis in the emerging new schools was in the arts and sciences and in the preparation of treatises.

Chart 124

The Introduction of Aristotle's Writings into Western Theology

TIME	BOOKS	NATURE OF THE INFLUENCE
1. Boethius (480–524)	*Categories* *Peri Hermenias*	Logic, Grammar (Philosophy as a tool of technical analysis)
2. c. 1100	*Prior and Posterior Analytics* *Topics* *Sophistical Arguments*	Logic, Grammar, Dialectics (Dialectics as a theological method)
3. 1175–1215	The remainder of his books	Aristotelian Content (Categories, content, and structure from *Physics, Metaphysics, Psychology,* and *Ethics*)

Western churchmen introduced Aristotle's writings to help prepare those who possessed the ability to defend the Christian faith. Islamic scholars had found Aristotle helpful in the defense of their religion; Thomas Aquinas saw in Aristotle's method a way to confront the adversary for the cause of Christ.

Chart 125

Scholastic Approaches to Knowing

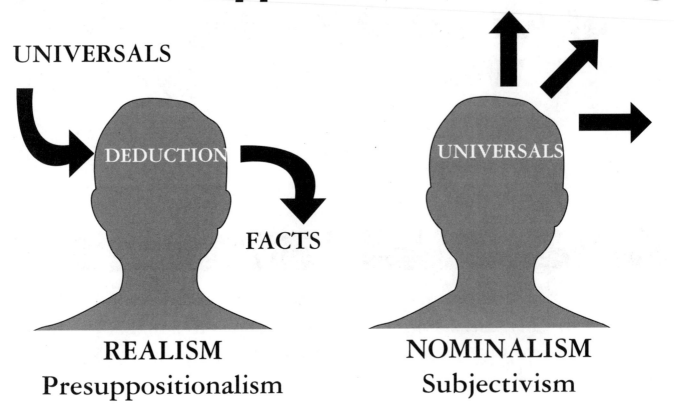

UNIVERSALS

DEDUCTION

FACTS

REALISM
Presuppositionalism

UNIVERSALS

NOMINALISM
Subjectivism

UNIVERSALS

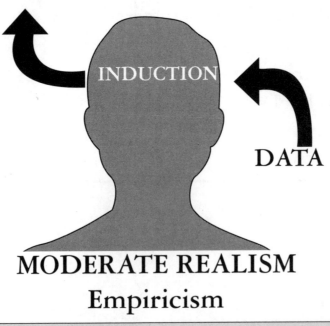

INDUCTION

DATA

MODERATE REALISM
Empiricism

A major discussion among Scholastics was the nature of knowing. The issue of *what* can be known was one not posed by Scholastics because of their deep commitments to the church and the Bible; the answer to the question of *how* one can know did come to have a profound impact on what can be known, but not in the medieval period.

Chart 126

Anselm and the Meaning of the Atonement

Substitution

"A Curse for us"

Galatians 3:13

The Scholastics' intellectual interest is readily seen in Anselm. Not only did he argue for the existence of God, he also demonstrated the rationality of Christ's atonement—the first such book-length rational explanation in the history of the church. Sin is an affront to God's honor; justice demands recompense by the perpetrator. Thus, mankind *must* pay for the sin of disobedience, yet they are incapable of rendering satisfaction to God, whose divine ground of forgiveness is his own perfect character. The solution: the divine/human Christ, who as a man identified with sinners by taking their sin and guilt into his own person so as to die in their place and who as God could endure divine wrath.

Chart 127

Abelard and the Meaning of the Atonement

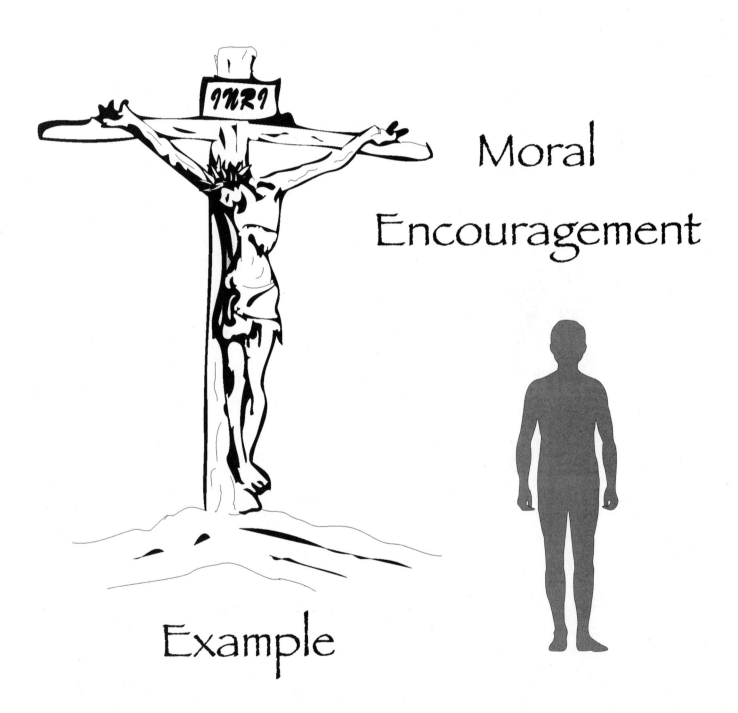

Moral

Encouragement

Example

While Anselm argued that the atonement has to do with God's justice (his righteousness demanding satisfaction or punishment), Abelard argued that the atonement pivots on the love of God. Christ's death is a demonstration of divine love, which should cause us to respond in obedience. Yet, a weak view of sin leads to a weak view of Christ's death on the cross, Abelard's critics argued.

Chart 128

The Anselmic and Abelardian Theories in Protestantism

ANSELMIC VIEW ⟷ ABELARDIAN VIEW

Lutherans	Socinians
Calvinists	Unitarians
Arminians	Religious Liberals
Wesleyans	
Amyraldians	

The view of divine substitution versus a benevolent demonstration represent two tendencies when it comes to interpreting Christ's death. Anselmic advocates stress that sin is such a devastation that only a divine substitute could ever adjudicate its effect, whereas Abelardian advocates see the substitutionary view as cruel, unjust, and unnecessary. In their view, Christ is the supreme human being who taught a simple moral message of love, only to be misunderstood and murdered.

Chart 129

Peter Lombard: The Source and Application of Merit

Increased merit culminating
in justification

Effects virtues in individuals by faith

Administered by the Spirit
through the sacraments

Based on the atonement of Christ

The prominence in late medieval theology of Peter Lombard's system of thought is established by the use of *The Four Sentences* in the training of churchmen in the emerging universities. He argued that grace is apportioned incrementally to the saint of God. God's grace causes the performance of good deeds, which cause greater degrees of grace to be granted, leading to complete grace. Justification (the fullest manifestation of grace) is actually a fruit of progressive sanctification, completed only after death.

Chart 130

Peter Lombard:
The Concept of Grace

Merit

Merit

Merit

Merit

Virtuous Acts
Grace or Charity
Prayer for Grace

For Lombard, grace and works are linked in a causative relationship: Grace always precedes merit. Grace is initially given through baptism, causing the remission of sins connected to Adam. Additional grace is given through the sacraments, leading to greater obedience that can culminate in final grace or justification. Lombard's theology confuses justification and sanctification. The insight that the grace of justification is instantaneously granted at the inception of the Christian's experience, needing no increase, is a biblical insight awaiting the Reformers in the sixteenth century.

Chart 131

Peter Lombard:
The Seven Sacraments as Means of Grace

1. Baptism

2. Confirmation

3. Eucharist

4. Penance

5. Unction

6. Orders

7. Matrimony

It was largely through the influence of Lombard that the medieval church agreed on seven sacraments, a teaching given official status at the Council of Florence (1438–1445). Five of the sacraments are performed only once: baptism, confirmation, unction, orders, and matrimony. Two (Eucharist and penance) are repeated often and along with baptism are the central "mysteries of grace." While each has a particular function, they cause an increase of justifying grace, leading to salvation or full grace.

Chart 132

Peter Lombard:
The Seven Sacraments Explained

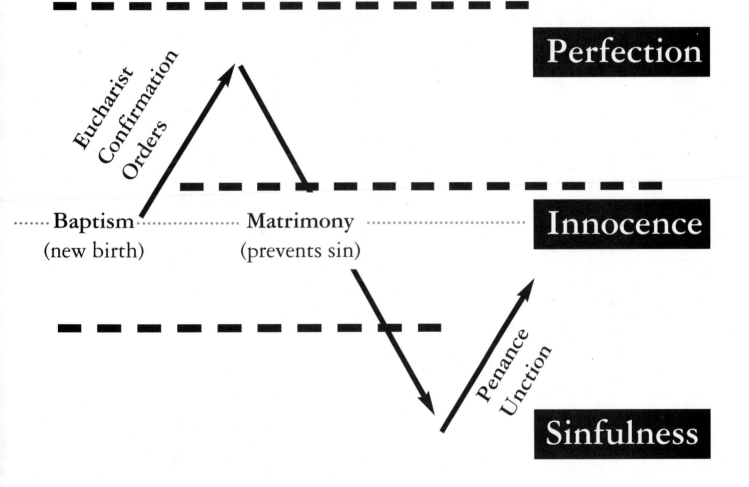

Perfection

Innocence

Baptism
(new birth)

Matrimony
(prevents sin)

Eucharist
Confirmation
Orders

Penance
Unction

Sinfulness

Baptism is the "new birth," delivering freedom from the guilt of Adam's sin as well as a weakened sinful propensity. The sacrament of matrimony is a gift that curbs the inordinate sexual attractions of the flesh by channeling these expressions in a sanctioned manner. Three sacraments function to increase grace, the most important being the Eucharist. Penance replenishes grace when a person is able to cooperate, while unction is offered only in a state of inability, namely, the threat of impending death, through the graces of the church. At death residual imperfections are removed in purgatory, and heaven is finally entered.

Chart 133

The History of the Doctrine of the Lord's Supper

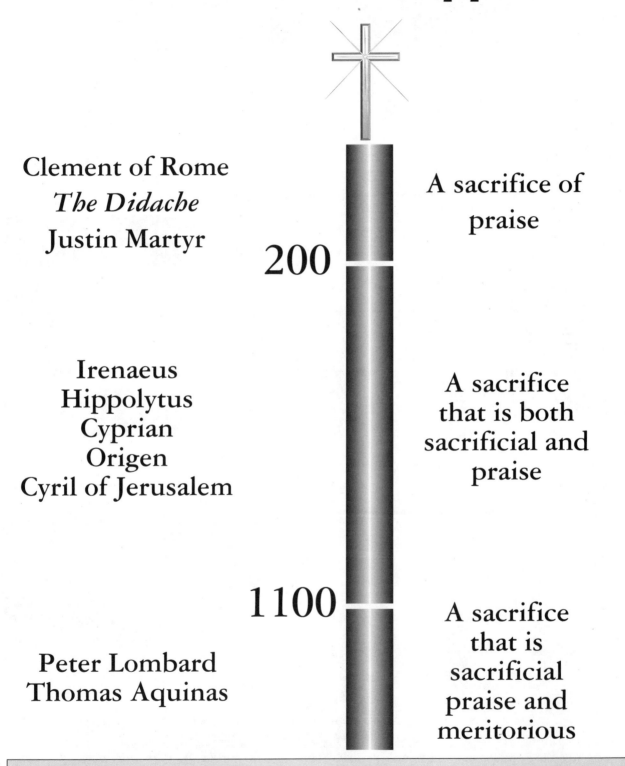

Clement of Rome
The Didache
Justin Martyr

200

A sacrifice of
praise

Irenaeus
Hippolytus
Cyprian
Origen
Cyril of Jerusalem

A sacrifice
that is both
sacrificial and
praise

1100

Peter Lombard
Thomas Aquinas

A sacrifice
that is
sacrificial
praise and
meritorious

The understanding of the Lord's Supper (Eucharist) gradually developed through the centuries. It was only in the later medievalists such as Lombard and Aquinas that the Eucharist was interpreted as providing meritorious grace. The church had consistently taught that Christ was truly present in the elements.

Chart 134

Transubstantiation:
The Roman Catholic View of the Lord's Table

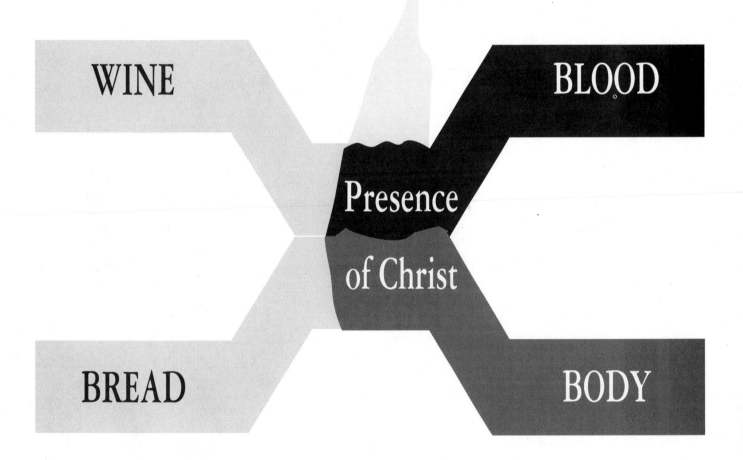

WINE

BLOOD

Presence

of Christ

BREAD

BODY

The meaning of the Eucharist was a key point of controversy between Roman Catholics and Protestants in the sixteenth century because the issue involved the nature of "salvation grace." Roman Catholics interpreted the Eucharist as the literal, physical presence of Christ in which the common elements of bread and wine were miraculously transformed into Christ's body and blood. Protestants objected to this and would also reject the ideas of incremental grace and merit so intrinsic to this view. The Eucharist, in this view, had the power to provide forgiveness of sins, thereby denigrating the finished work of Christ.

Chart 135

The Accomplishments of Christ:
A Treasury of Merit

Purchased:
A Treasury of Merit

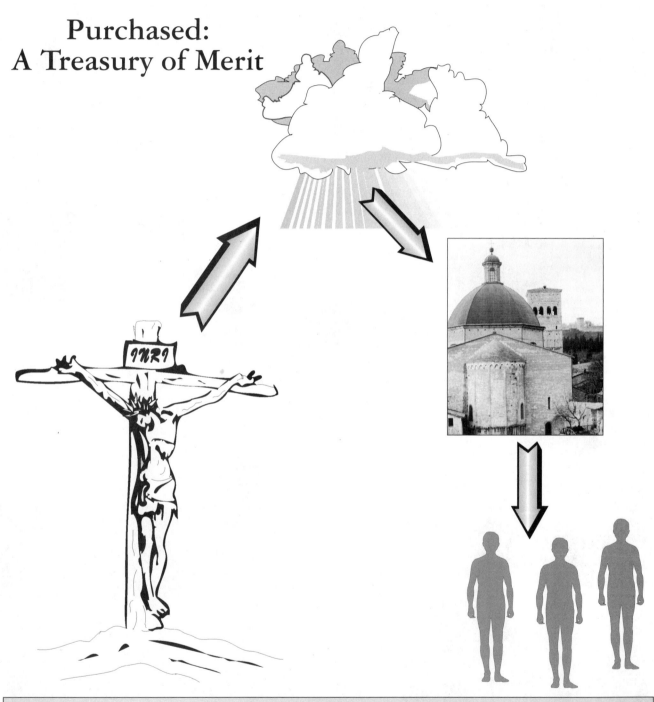

The late medieval sacramental view of the benefits of Christ's death included his substitutionary work, yet with a twist that would differ from the Reformers' view. Christ's penalty-bearing death won the grace sufficient for the forgiveness of the sins of the world, but this grace was not directly given to anyone. The keys to this treasury of grace were given to the church, which would dispense grace through the sacraments. When a person had enough grace accredited to their "salvation account," they obtained final justification. Salvation is by grace, based upon the merit of Christ, but this merit is acquired through the graces of the church.

Chart 136

Thomas Aquinas and Merit through an Increase of Grace

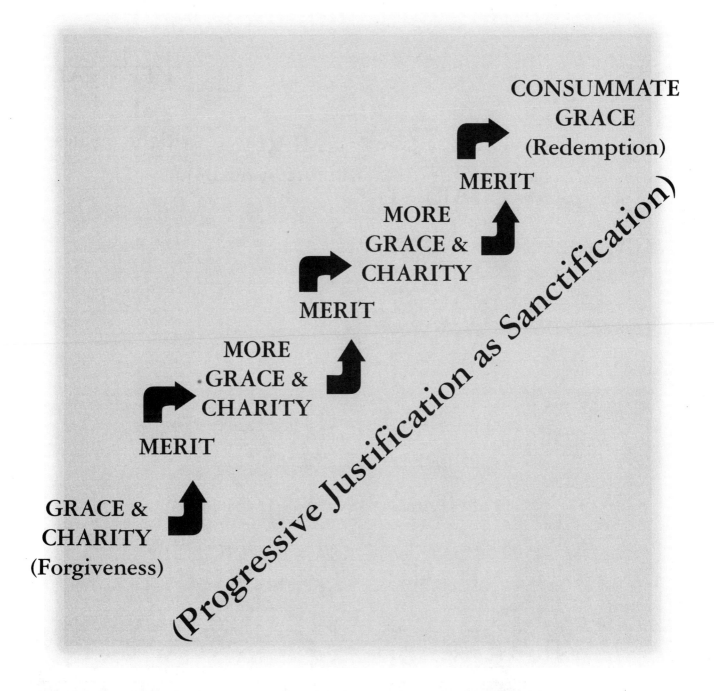

CONSUMMATE
GRACE
(Redemption)

MERIT

MORE
GRACE &
CHARITY

MERIT

MORE
GRACE &
CHARITY

MERIT

GRACE &
CHARITY
(Forgiveness)

(Progressive Justification as Sanctification)

Thomas Aquinas was the greatest of all medieval scholars. He saw grace and cooperation more intrinsically interrelated and inseparable than Peter Lombard did. In his view salvation is the fruit of progressive justification; grace causes an increase of works, or piety, that is rewarded with merit, which causes an increase of grace leading to final salvation. Here again, grace and works are intricately connected.

Chart 137

Thomas Aquinas: Divine Redemption and Merit

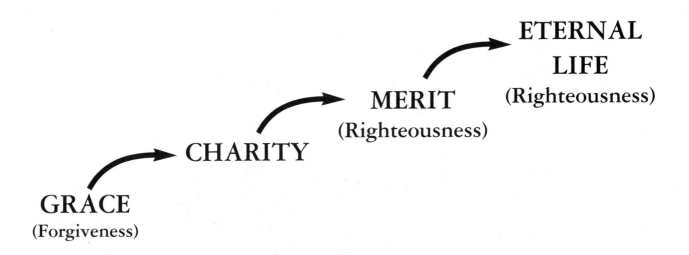

"The meriting of eternal life depends principally on charity."

"Our merit is the secondary cause."

"A man merits an increase of grace by each and every meritorious action."

"He cannot merit the first grace."

Aquinas viewed justification as a process in which sin is gradually overcome and displaced by the fruit of the Spirit through the increase of ability obtained through the sacraments. While the Reformers would appreciate his emphasis on the priority of grace, they would be disappointed at his failure to see justifying grace as granted fully at the saint's first experience of grace. Moreover, they would reject his notion that the sacraments functioned to deliver the grace of salvation.

Chart 138

Thomas Aquinas and Justification:
Forgiveness without Righteousness

Justification
(saving grace, righteousness)

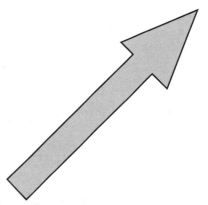

Sanctification
(cumulative grace through merit)

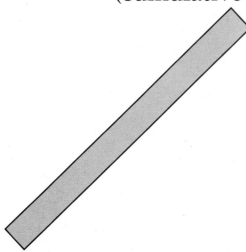

"Man is justified by faith, not in the sense that he merits justification by believing, but in the sense that he believes while he is being justified."

Remission of Sin
(conditional forgiveness)

Aquinas interpreted salvation as a process that was only determined when final grace or justification was obtained. Baptism, the removal of the guilt of Adam's first sin, does not ensure final redemption; it simply renders one "savable" should grace be increased sufficiently. Grace is increased through the sacraments, as merit is progressively accumulated, and grace is finalized in justification.

Chart 139

Thomas Aquinas:
The Steps to Salvation

**The
End**

Reward of
eternal life as
a just due

**The
Result**

**The
Beginning**

Moral
cooperation:
doing the best
one can with
the aid of grace

The gratuitous
infusion of
grace

Another way to describe the progress of salvation is to view it in steps. The beginning of salvation is rooted in the infusion of divine grace, which results in the ability to cooperate with God. This effort is manifested in the performance of the sacraments and moral obedience in general. Increased merit is eventually rewarded with eternal life. The Reformers, on the other hand, would see God's grace as imputed instantaneously, not progressively infused.

Chart 140

Thomas Aquinas and Transubstantiation

"He is then able to bring about not merely a changing of form . . . but the changing of the whole being of a thing, so that the complete substance of this is changed into the complete substance of that. And this actually happens by divine power in this sacrament. The complete substance of the bread is converted into the complete substance of Christ's body, and the complete substance of the vine into the complete substance of Christ's blood. Hence this change is not a formal change, but a substantial one. It does not belong to the natural kinds of change, and it can be called by a name proper to itself–'transubstantiation.'"

Thomas Aquinas
Summa 3a. 75,74.

In Thomas's understanding of the Eucharist, the bread and wine are miraculously transformed into the actual body and blood of Christ. As such, they possess a cleansing efficacy—a point strenuously opposed by the Reformers because it contradicted their understanding of grace as instantaneously imputed. In the Reformers' objection to infused, progressive grace, they focused their attack on the church's faulty view of the Eucharist.

Chart 141

Thomas Aquinas: The Role of Baptism

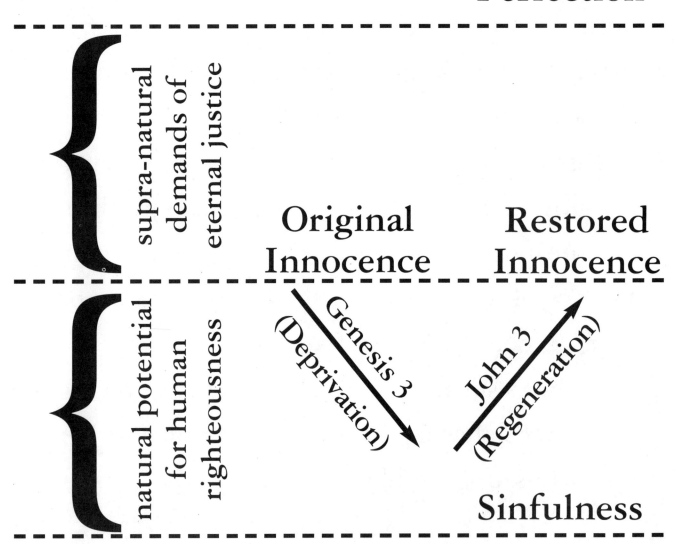

Perfection

{ supra-natural demands of eternal justice

Original Innocence

Restored Innocence

{ natural potential for human righteousness

Genesis 3 (Deprivation)

John 3 (Regeneration)

Sinfulness

Aquinas argued that mankind fell from innocence with Adam and was deprived of original righteousness. Thus, a child is born into the world sinful by declaration, though not by action. Baptism washes away this sinfulness and restores the child to innocence. The gap between innocence and perfection is breached through the grace of the sacraments.

Chart 142

The Importance of Thomas Aquinas in the Roman Catholic Tradition

"St. Thomas Aquinas may be said to have been present at all the Ecumenical Councils of the Church after his time, presiding as it were, by his invisible presence and his living teachings over their deliberations and decrees; but that greatest and most special honor was given to the Angelic Doctor at the Council of Trent, when, during its sessions, together with the Bible and the formal decrees of the Sovereign Pontiffs, the Fathers of the Council had the open *Summa* placed upon the altar so that thence they might draw counsels, arguments, and oracles. This was a singular honor and praise accorded to St. Thomas which was not given to any of the Fathers or other Doctors of the Church."

Pope Leo XIII
August 4, 1879
Encyclical Aeterni Patris

The importance of Aquinas in the history of the church can hardly be overestimated. His perspectives on grace, salvation, and merit form the foundation of Roman Catholic doctrine as specified at the Council of Trent (1545–1563).

Chart 143

Thomas Aquinas
and the Reformers:
Views of Justification Compared

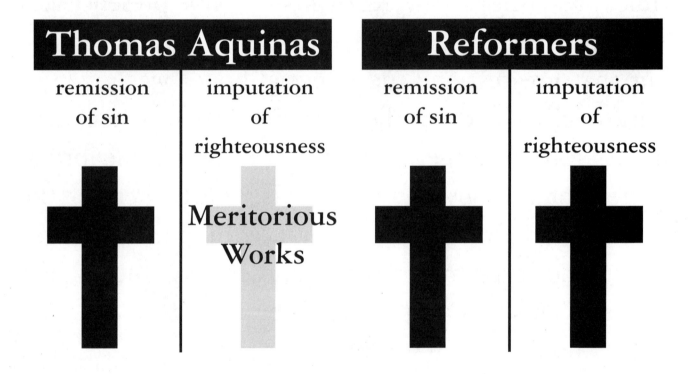

Thomas Aquinas		Reformers	
remission of sin	imputation of righteousness	remission of sin	imputation of righteousness
	Meritorious Works		

When we compare Thomas's and the Reformers' views of justification, the differences become clear. The former viewed "salvation grace" as a progressive accomplishment for the saint through the merit of good works (though that merit is caused by the grace of God). The Reformers viewed the grace of salvation as separate from the sacraments, which are the means of *sanctifying* grace but not of justifying grace. Justifying grace, according to the Reformers, admits no increase because it is fully given at salvation. Justifying grace is imputed; it is reckoned by God.

Chart 144

William of Ockham and Gabriel Biel:
The Steps to Salvation

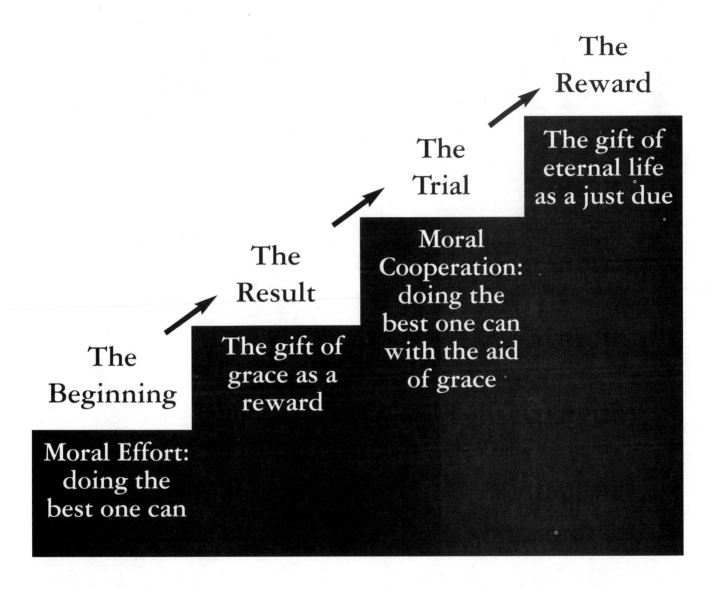

The Reward

The gift of eternal life as a just due

The Trial

Moral Cooperation: doing the best one can with the aid of grace

The Result

The gift of grace as a reward

The Beginning

Moral Effort: doing the best one can

Some teachers in the church (William of Ockham and Gabriel Biel, in particular) went beyond Lombard and Aquinas in explaining the relationship between grace, human response, merit, and salvation. Their teachings represent an acceptance of Pelagius, Augustine's fifth-century opponent. The cause of salvation is rooted in self-endeavor, which moves God to grant grace; the acquisition of grace causes a higher degree of obedience, which leads to eternal life as a just reward. The issue is not divine grace from beginning to end, as taught by the Reformers, or even a grace-induced cooperation, but salvation caused by human effort assisted by God's grace. Roman Catholics and Protestants alike rejected this dangerous drift into Pelagianism.

Chart 145

The Reformation Traditions:
Different Views of the Past

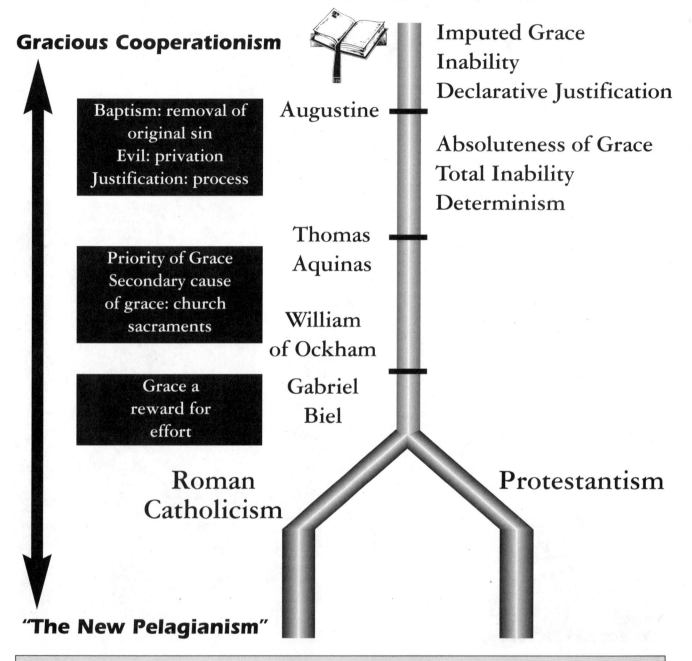

Gracious Cooperationism

Imputed Grace
Inability
Declarative Justification

Augustine

Absoluteness of Grace
Total Inability
Determinism

Baptism: removal of original sin
Evil: privation
Justification: process

Thomas Aquinas

Priority of Grace
Secondary cause of grace: church sacraments

William of Ockham

Gabriel Biel

Grace a reward for effort

Roman Catholicism

Protestantism

"The New Pelagianism"

Despite serious disagreements in many areas of doctrine, both Roman Catholics and Protestants agreed that any necessary reform should not be along the lines of Pelagianism; yet they could not agree on what position to take. Thus, two movements emerged, often antithetical in the extreme, yet fashioned out of the same centuries of Christian history. In rejecting late medieval Pelagianism, Roman Catholic scholars accepted the Thomist doctrine of grace and sacraments, as well as Augustine's teachings on baptism, the definition of sin as the absence of righteousness (a negation or privation only), and justification as a process. The Reformers went beyond this to other elements in Augustine, namely, his emphasis on the absolute necessity of grace and (at least for some Reformers) his teachings on election and determinism. They also pointed to the biblical (Pauline) emphasis on imputed (not infused) grace, human inability, and (most crucially) declarative justification.

Chart 146

The Fracturing of the Church:
The Need for Reform

The Church on the Eve of the Reformation

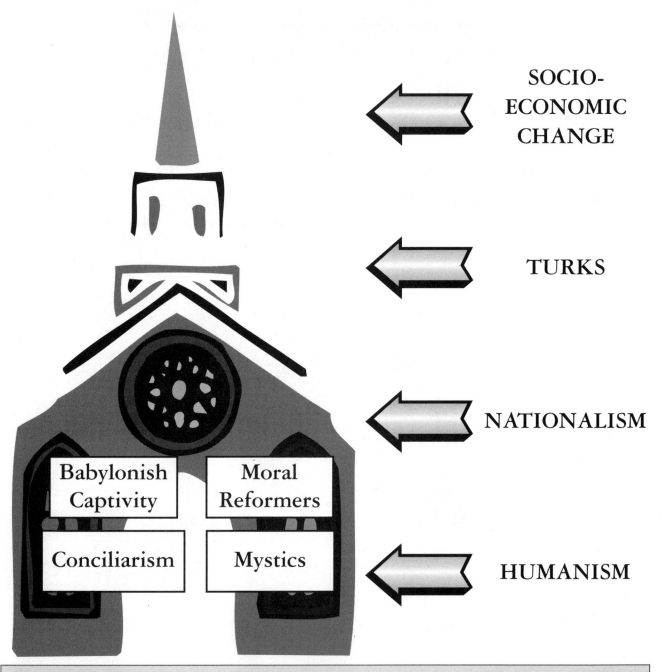

SOCIO-ECONOMIC CHANGE

TURKS

NATIONALISM

HUMANISM

Babylonish Captivity

Moral Reformers

Conciliarism

Mystics

The causes of the division that would culminate in the reform movements of the sixteenth century are numerous and complex. Within the church, Martin Luther's 1520 document called the "Babylonish Captivity of the Church" raised the issues of the sacraments and the authority of the church, while the conciliar movement asserted that general councils of the church had greater authority than the pope. Mystics turned away from the church toward a inward, private quest for meaning apart from sacraments and papal decrees. Voices pointing out the corruption of the church increased. Outside the church factors such as socioeconomic changes, threats posed by the Ottoman Turks, and the advances of nationalism and humanism brought the authority of the church into question.

Chart 147

How the Reformation Came About:
Three Essentials

MILIEU

trouble inside and outside

MESSAGE

sola scriptura ✝ *sola gratia* *sola fide*

MEANS

printing press

Viewed negatively, the factors calling for reform were rooted in the decline of the prestige of the church as evidenced by the rise of clergy error, immorality, and greed. Viewed positively, the Reformation was occasioned by the discovery of the teachings of the Bible after centuries of increasing distortion. At the same time, the invention of the printing press and the rise of literacy in the emerging middle classes provided the means for the dissemination of new and radical ideas.

Chart 148

The Controversy over Papal versus Conciliar Authority

PAPALISTS	CONCILIARISTS	RADICALS
Supreme Authority = POPE	Supreme Authority = COUNCIL	Supreme Authority ≠ POPE ≠ COUNCIL
• Giles of Rome • James of Viterbo	• Conrad of Gelnhausen • Henry of Langenstein • Jean Gerson • Pierre d' Ailly	• Wycliffe • Huss • Luther

During the centuries leading up to the Reformation, the question of authority in the church evoked strident discussion; in fact, the failure to resolve the issue was one of the major contributing causes of the Reformation. Some believed that final authority rested in the papal office, others that the councils of the church held the final authority, and still others that all authority resided in the holy Scriptures.

Chart 149

The Latin Vulgate:
The Need for New Translations

Matthew 4:17 and Penance
 do penance (outward practice)
 repent (inward psychological state)

Luke 1:28 and Mary
 grata plena (full of grace, or favored one)

Ephesians 5:31–32 and Marriage
 sacramentum (sacrament)
 mysterion (mystery)

The humanist movement brought a renewal of the study of the ancient sources that undergirded the claims of the church. The Latin Vulgate (Jerome's fifth-century translation) needed to be revised. Words had changed meaning, and the knowledge of the Bible text had increased. Many were claiming that errors in the church could be traced a faulty understanding of the Scriptures. Is penance a thing to be done (an outward practice), or is it an inward state of mind? Is Mary the favored one because of the privilege given her to bear the Savior, or is she favored because of intrinsic qualities? Is marriage a mystery, an echo of the relationship of Christ and his church, or is it a sacrament, a means of grace?

Chart 150

John Wycliffe:
A Voice for Reform

Born:	c. 1320
Place of Birth:	Yorkshire, England
Died:	1384
Educated at:	Oxford University
Place of Ministry:	Oxford, England
Position:	Professor
Contribution:	Translated Bible into English
Major Works:	*On Civil Lordship* *On the Mass* *On the Pastoral Office*

In the centuries before the Reformation, there were numerous voices, John Wycliffe among them, who called for a return to the Bible as the sole authority in religion. Highly critical of the papacy and various church abuses, this Oxford teacher translated the Bible into English. When John Huss was burned for heresy in 1415, Wycliffe was disinterred and his bones burned. Such was the hostility of the church to reform in the fifteenth century.

Chart 151

The Meaning of the Renaissance

1. Revival of Classical Learning

2. Methodology (not Philosophy)

3. Not a Forerunner of Modern Democratic Liberalism

The Reformation was a fruit of the Renaissance, a grand intellectual movement of the fourteenth century that featured classical learning, the rise of the university, and a greater emphasis on methodology than on philosophy. Although the Renaissance did bear fruit in the origins of the seventeenth-century Enlightenment, it should not be identified with modern "democratic liberalism" or modern humanism, with its rejection of the church as an authority over the conscience.

Chart 152

The Renaissance Academies in Italy

The Renaissance flourished in the emerging academies of Italy, where scholars from Constantinople reintroduced ancient texts that were the foundational sources of Christian teachings. The academies became significant for the Reformation, as students came to realize that the church was teaching things that were not rooted in the most ancient sources.

Chart 153

Scholasticism and Renaissance Humanism Compared

	Scholasticism (1100–1300)	Humanism (1300–1500)
1. Major area of study:	Theology	Science, Medicine, Theology
2. Questions:	Answered in Theology	No Resolution Necessary
3: Truth:	Church-based	Nostalgic, Free, Challenging
4: Focus:	Otherworldly	Practical, Immediate

Scholasticism differed considerably from the Renaissance humanist movement that was a key factor in the fracturing of the late medieval church. Areas of study broadened in the Renaissance, the purpose of the endeavor was radically different, and truth was not as tightly connected with the teachings of the church.

Chart 154

The Medieval View of History

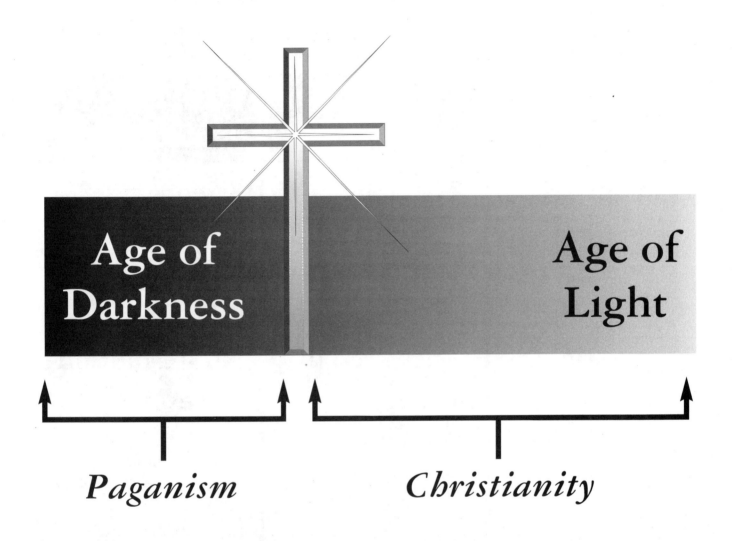

Age of Darkness

Age of Light

Paganism

Christianity

Continuity of Truth

As the Reformation neared, the church viewed the Middle Ages as a period of advance because the church had directed the affairs of society; Renaissance scholars, on the other hand, viewed it as a dark period because the church had suppressed free inquiry and promoted error.

Chart 155

The Renaissance View of History

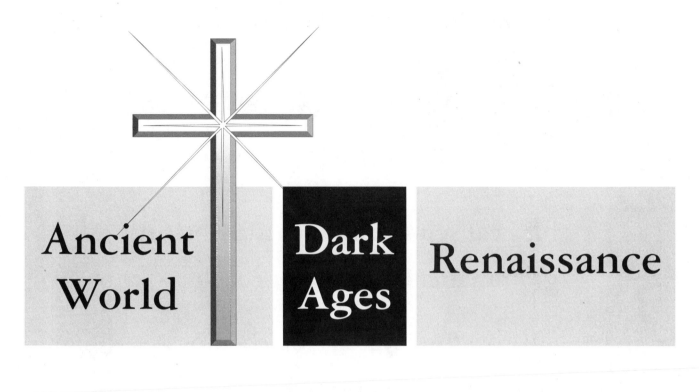

Ancient World | Dark Ages | Renaissance

Light   *Darkness*   *Light*

Continuity of Truth ------------------------Continuity of Truth

Chart 156

The Need for Reform:
Agreement between Luther and Erasmus

The need for a new type of...

- biblical scholarship: the historical, grammatical, literal approach

- approach to systematic theology: an exegetical approach

- popular piety: Bible oriented

- clergy for the church

- hierarchy in the church

While both Luther and Erasmus recognized the need for reform in the church and for a return to the Bible by a more thoughtful, caring clergy, they held widely different views on the issues of the nature of sin, grace, sacraments, and merit. Those differences spawned two reforming movements: Roman Catholicism and Protestantism.

Chart 157

The Conflict between Luther and Erasmus

"Their debate, seemingly narrow and obscure, actually involved the most fundamental discussion of nature and destiny."

Steven Ozment,
The Age of Reform, 290

Chart 158

The Failure of the Church on the Eve of the Reformation

"The failure of the late medieval church to provide a theology and spirituality that could satisfy and discipline religious hearts and minds was the most important religious pre-condition of the Reformation."

Steven Ozment,
The Age of Reform, 203

Chart 159